EDWARD CHASZAR

THE INTERNATIONAL PROBLEM OF NATIONAL MINORITIES

THIRD EDITION
REVISED AND ENLARGED

1999

MATTHIAS CORVINUS PUBLISHING

Toronto - Buffalo

TABLE OF CONTENTS

Table of contents.. i

Preface to the third edition............................... 1

I. The Problem of National Minorities Before
and After the Paris Peace Treaties of 1947........................ 4

II. Can the United Nations Protect the
Rights of Minorities? 18

III. International Protection of Minorities in the
Middle East: A Status Report 34

IV. Trianon and the Problem of National Minorities 52

V. The Ethnic Principle and National Boundaries
(A Case study of the Czechoslovak-Hungarian
Border Dispute of 1938) 64

Appendices:

Rights of Persons Belonging to National, Ethnic,
Religious and Linguistic Minorities (Commission on
Human Rights, 34th session,
Draft Declaration proposed by Yugoslavia) 80

Text of the Draft Declaration as adopted in first reading
(Commission on Human Rights, 1990) 83

Text of the Draft Declaration as adopted in second reading
(Commission on Human Rights, 1992) 88

Proposal for a European Convention for the
Protection of Minorities (adopted by the European
Cimmission for Democtacy, on 8 February 1991)........... 93

i

Recommendation 1201 (1993) on an additional
protocol on the rights of minorities to the
European Convention on Human Rights 105

Framework Convention for the Protection of
National Minorities (Council of Europe, 1994) 113

Explanatory report on the Framework Convention
for the Protection of National Minorities 125

European Charter of Local Self-Government
(Council of Europe, 1985) 147

Document of the Copenhagen Meeting of the
Conference on the Human Dimension of
the CSCE (1990) 157

High Commissioner on National Minorities
(CSCE Document, Helsinki, July 1992) 164

High Commissioner on National Minorities
(Washington D.C., June 1993) 171

Central European Initiative Instrument for the
Protection of Minority Rights (1994) 178

Draft of an International Convention on the
Protection of National or Ethnic Groups or Minorities
(by the International Institute for Ethnic Group Rights
and Regionalism, 1978) 189

Basic Principles of a Rights of Nationalities
(by the Federal Union of European Nationalities;
Unanimously adopted by the 17th Congress of the
FUEN in its sitting at Abenra on 22 May 1967) 199

Act LXXVII of 1993 on the Rights of National and
Ethnic Minorities (Republic of Hungary,
Office of National and Ethnic Minorities) 202

PREFACE TO THE THIRD EDITION

When the first edition of this modest collection of studies, concerning the international protection of minorities, was published in 1988 by the Minority Rights Research Program at Indiana University of Pennsylvania, the political world was an altogether different place. Although signs of change in the Soviet Union, and in some parts of its Central and Eastern European domain, were already discernible, the conduct of international relations was still geared largely to the existence of a bipolar world structure.

In retrospect one may say that the bipolar world presented a certain degree of stability and predictability. Local disturbances, like civil strife in some countries, as well as ethnic conflict in others, could be handled and contained by diplomacy, or limited use of force. Yet, under the surface there existed forces to be revealed later, namely latent nationalism, the rising of hitherto subdued - or suppressed - ethnic consciousness, and violent ethnic strife, mostly growing out of discrimination against minorities by majorities.

Other than occasional references to the problems of minorities at CSCE conferences, that is, at the follow-up meetings to the 1975 Helsinki Accords, there was no systematic approach to these problems, with one exception. The United Nations Commission on Human Rights in Geneva was, since 1978, grappling with the "Rights of Persons Belonging to National, Ethnic, Religious and Linguistic Minorities."

It was, however, not until the 1992 session of the Commission that the Draft Declaration dealing with these rights was finally approved and went on for adoption by the U.N. General Assembly in December, 1992 .

In the meantime other international organizations also took up the task of finding some solution to the problem. In view of increased ethnic strife, erupting in bloodshed after the dissolution of the Soviet Union, and the break-up of the

1

Socialist Federal Republic of Yugoslavia, the task took on added importance. The Council of Europe, CSCE (Conference on Security and Co-operation in Europe), the European Parliament, the Central European Initiative, and others started to grapple with the problem of minority rights, and began to produce recommendations, resolutions, declarations, agreements and protocols to address the problem. (Several of these instruments are reproduced in the Appendix.)

As for the studies collected in this volume, they were written between the years 1977 and 1988, with the intention of alerting the public of the plight of national, ethnic, religious and linguistic minorities in different parts of the world, especially in East Central Europe and in the Middle East. The unifying theme of the studies is the problem of granting rights to minorities to preserve their identity, and the international protection of these rights. Renewed interest in the subject makes it feasible to publish a third, revised and expanded edition, despite the fact that some of the studies selected for this edition overlap both in scope and in content. The order in which the studies are presented has no particular significance, but their original place of publication merits listing for the purpose of acknowledgement.

The first study was originally presented at the Duquesne History Forum (Pittsburgh, Pennsylvania) in the fall of 1980. Subsequently it was published in the Fall, 1981, issue of **Nationalities Papers** (Volume IX, Number 2).

The second study was originally presented at the Annual Convention of the International Studies Association in 1987, and subsequently rewritten for publication in the Spring, 1988, issue of **Proteus**, devoted in its entirety to the work of the United Nations. (Volume 5, Number 1, Copyright 1988 by **Proteus**, Shippensburg, Pennsylvania.)

The third study was presented at the Duquesne History Forum in the fall of 1984, and published in the Spring, 1986, issue of the **Middle East Review** (Vol.XVIII, Number 2).

The article on "Trianon and the Problem of National Minorities" was written for, and published in, War and Society in East Central Europe, Volume VI, Essays on World War I: **Total War and Peacemaking**, a Case Study on Trianon. Bela Kiraly, Peter Pastor and Ivan Sanders, editors. (Social

Science Monographs, Brooklyn College Press; Copyright 1982 by Atlantic Research and Publications.)

The fifth article, dealing with "The Ethnic Principle and National Boundaries: A Case Study of the Czechoslovak-Hungarian Border Dispute of 1938" was written for, and published in, the Belgian quarterly **Documentation sur l'Europe Centrale**, Volume XV, Number 4 (1977).

The expanded Appendix contains a selection of public documents related to the rights of minorities.

The author is grateful to the editors and publishers for their kind permission to reprint the articles, and to the Matthias Corvinus Publishing Company for undertaking this third, revised and expanded edition.

Edward Chaszar
Professor Emeritus

Indiana University of Pennsylvania
Summer, 1999

I. THE PROBLEM OF
NATIONAL MINORITIES BEFORE AND
AFTER THE PARIS PEACE TREATIES OF 1947*

* Presented at the 14th Annual Duquesne History Forum, Pittsburgh, Pa., October 27, 1980

The purpose of this paper is to compare briefly the situation of national minorities in Europe before and after the Paris Peace Treaties of 1947. More particularly, to contrast the League of Nations system of minority protection with the lack of a similar system within the United Nations framework, and recent attempts to remedy this shortcoming.

As a historical note, it should be registered here that concern with the protection of minorities originated in the religious sphere. Historically, international efforts to protect religious minorities against persecution took the form of ad hoc intervention by states on behalf of their co-religionists in other countries. Later practice included guarantees of freedom of religion for inhabitants of territories transferred to other countries by voluntary or forced cession. Occasionally, when religious division was identical with national division, such guarantees protected an entire nationality within a state.

The first express recognition and international guarantee of the rights of national minorities is found in the Final Act of the Congress of Vienna, in which Russia, Prussia, and Austria undertook to respect the nationality of their Polish subjects.1

The systematic protection of national minorities did not become a reality until the end of World War I and the establishment of the League of Nations. Even this system was limited in scope and applied only to special cases. A more comprehensive system of wider application is still missing today.

The League of Nations System of Minority Protection

The century preceding the outbreak of World War I was characterized by the spreading and intensification of national consciousness, on the one hand, and by the determined, sometimes ruthless, campaigns for the suppression of national movements, on the other. Consequently, at the outbreak of the war the national question was one of the major unresolved problems in international relations. When the war ended, the principle of national self-determination was brought to the fore. The Paris Peace Conference "allowed and sponsored the operation of that principle in a number of cases, chiefly where it worked to the disadvantage of the defeated powers, but admitted other factors as coordinate and, in some cases, overriding elements in the determination of frontiers. The principle of 'one nation, one state' was not realized to the full extent permitted by the ethnographic configuration of Europe, but it was approximated more closely than ever before."2

Still, the redrawing of the frontiers of the great polyglot empires of Eastern and Central Europe, and the limited reshuffling of populations, did by no means solve the problem of national minorities. The powers, in violation of proclaimed Wilsonian principles, handed over masses of people to alien sovereignties. Inis L. Claude, Jr., estimates the number to have been between 25 and 30 million, and a British authority on the question of national self-determination wrote as follows: "it was ironic that a settlement supposed to have been largely determined by the principle of nationality should have produced a state like Czechoslovakia, with minorities amounting to 34.7 per cent of its population, quite apart from the question of the doubtful identity of nationality between Czechs and Slovaks. Poland was not much better off with minorities amounting to 30.4 per cent, or Roumania, with 25 per cent."3

This should explain why, as Clemenceau pointed out to Paderewski in his oft-quoted letter justifying the imposition of restrictions upon Poland's handling of national minorities, the powers felt a solemn obligation to protect those peoples whose future minority status was determined by their decision. A plan for the international protection of national minorities appeared to be the only solution, and such a plan was evolved out of a multiplicity of conflicting interests and points of view, and utilizing an unprecedented set of international machinery, the League of Nations.4

The basis of the League of Nations system for the international protection of minorities consisted of a series of treaties, declarations, and conventions whereby particular states accepted provisions relating to the treatment of minority groups and at the same time recognized the League as guarantor.5

Although different in form, these instruments aimed at safeguarding the rights of "racial, religious or linguistic minorities." And the architects of the system made it clear that they regarded this designation as synonymous with "national minorities."6

The rights guaranteed to national minorities in the treaty-bound states fell into two categories: the rights of individuals as such, and the rights of individuals as members of a minority group. The safeguarding of the first category of rights demanded a system of negative equality - protection against discrimination. The second category required in addition a regime of "positive equality" - provisions for the equal opportunity of minorities to "preserve and develop their national culture and consciousness."7 Nevertheless, these were still individual rights, arising out of membership in a minority and facilitating the maintenance and development of group life. Wilson and his fellow architects were too much imbued with the individualist traditions of liberalism to accept the concept of "group rights." The documents mentioned carefully avoided terminology from which it might have been inferred that minorities as corporate units were the intended beneficiaries of the system.8 Claude notes only few exceptions, such as Articles 9 and 10 of the Polish minority Treaty, which could be interpreted as indirectly granting recognition to groups per se.

This cautious interpretation of Claude concerning the nature of minority rights is not shared by all. On the contrary, some say that the rights protected by the League were, at least in part, rights accorded to minorities as groups. Thus, André Mandelstam in his La Protection des Minorités distinguishes between "droits reconnus aux membres des minorités à titre individuel" - religious liberty, freedom of using their own language, freedom of education in their own language, freedom of association - and "droits reconnus aux minorités comme entités collectives" - proportional representation in elective bodies, and autonomy.9

The League guarantee was collective. The task of enforcing the obligations of the concerned states was assigned to the organization, more specifically to the Council. In addition, although judicial procedures were available through the Permanent Court of International Justice, the guarantee as established was basically political in nature. It was part of a larger system designed to facilitate the maintenance of international peace.

In order to discharge its functions as a guarantor, the Council of the League developed certain operating procedures empirically (one might say "on a trial by error" method), starting with the suggestions contained in the Tittoni Report of 1920, and concluding with the 1929 report and recommendations of a special committee headed by Adatci, the Japanese representative, who served as the Council's Rapporteur on minority questions.10

It its final form the procedure consisted of five successive steps, namely:

a. Acceptance of Petitions [from minorities],
b. Communications to the Government concerned for any Observations,
c. Communication to the Members of the Council,
d. Examination by the Committee of Three [Council Members],
e. Replies to Petitioners.

Given the stringent qualifications that had to be met for each successive step and the half-hearted support the system enjoyed in the Council, this so called "petition system" functioned with limited success. Its failures and deficiencies were numerous. According to one of its many critics: "It is impossible to maintain that the minorities obtained an adequate and impartial hearing of their grievances and demands, or prompt, effective, and reliable measures of protection . . . The League system was superior to possible alternative arrangements relying exclusively upon internal constitutional guarantees of minority rights, or resting upon bilateral agreements unsupported by an international guarantee, or leaving the protection of minorities dependent upon the unregulated and capricious intervention of kin-states; but it was unable to solve the difficult problem with which it came to grips."11

Basically the League system was unpopular with all those concerned for a variety of reasons. The minority states disliked it because it limited their "sovereign rights." The minorities disliked it, because it was cumbersome and did not provide the protection desired. The kin-states were dissatisfied with the system, because they were excluded from it altogether. Moreover, it was a limited system rather than a general one, which proved to be very irksome to those who were placed under its obligations, while other nations - even though possessing minorities - were totally excluded. Thus, while Czechoslovakia for one was willing to cooperate, Poland was resentful and in 1934 produced a statement that amounted to a virtual denunciation of minority obligations. On September 13, 1934, Colonel Beck announced to the Assembly of the League that "pending the introduction of a general and uniform system for the protection of minorities, his Government was compelled to refuse, as from that day, all co-operation with the international organizations in the matter of supervision of the application by Poland of the system of minority protection."12

Following this declaration, the League system of minority protection became increasingly ineffectual, until it was ultimately swept away by the events of W. W. II.

The Paris Peace Treaties of 1947 and the United Nations System

As the League system of minority protection eroded, so did the hope of a functioning collective security system. Starting with the Manchurian incident and continuing with the Italo-Ethiopian war, it became evident that war had not been eliminated as the ultimate fact of international life. This, in turn, affected the position of national minorities vitally; they were soon regarded as potentially subversive elements by the states to which they owed formal allegiance and became suspect as possible allies of the states to which they were related by ethnic

8

ties

Indeed, World War II proved the above suspicion to be true in a number of instances. Hence, the case for protecting minorities grew weaker and weaker, while the case for reducing the number of national minorities, or eliminating them altogether, was strengthened. The Polish Government in exile announced categorically that "Poland would never again accept a Minorities Treaty," while the prestigious President Benes asserted that the League system "had broken down and could not be renewed." Anyway, he preferred the "transfer" (meaning expulsion) of all or most of the minorities from the State of which has was President, and suggested that any protection of the minorities in the future should consists "primarily in the defense of human rights and not of national rights."13

The solution of expulsion is said to have come quite naturally to Stalin, nor did Churchill have qualms about it. On the contrary, he told the House of Commons (after agreeing at Yalta to the westward shift of Poland's borders) that "expulsion was the method which, so far as we have been able to see, will be the most satisfactory and lasting. There will be no mixture of populations to cause endless trouble. . . A clean sweep will be made."14 The Potsdam Conference in the summer of 1945 agreed to "population transfer."

There are, of course, several methods for the solution of the problem of minorities. One possible solution is by moral transformation: assimilation, and cultural pluralism. Another solution might be reached by physical elimination: frontier revision, transfer, or self-determination. All of these seem to have been considered at one time or another during the war years. The conference which met in Paris in 1946 to make peace with the exbelligerents other than Germany, favored the policy of forced transfer (expulsion), with the single modification that Czechoslovakia was to abandon its proposed unilateral expulsion of its Hungarian minority in favor of a negotiated bilateral exchange. The Conference also expressed its satisfaction that Italy and Austria were able to handle their minority problem on a bilateral basis. On the whole, the proceedings at Paris were characterized by the de-internationalization of the minority problem. What national minorities were to be left after the various forced negotiated

9

population transfers, were no longer the responsibility of the international community. The troublesome problem was being handed back to the states concerned.

In fact, the great powers opposed granting to any surviving minorities such rights as they had enjoyed under the League system. Nor did they attempt to have any new obligations inserted in the Peace Treaties, "with the single exception that the British Delegation insisted on the inclusion in the Hungarian and Romanian Treaties of a clause borrowed from the U.N. Charter, prohibiting discrimination against nationals on the ground of their sex, race, language or religion; it did this, as the British Delegate frankly avowed, in the interest of the Jews."15 The Conference, however, failed to develop any methods of enforcement. An Australian proposal for a European Court of Justice to supervise the observance of human rights in former Axis countries was rejected on the ground that it was a task for the United Nations to create such institutions.

The United Nations:
Human Rights and the Rights of Minorities

The framers of the United Nations Charter accepted the idea that the protection of the minorities should take the form of "the defense of human rights and not of national rights." There is no mention of the problem in the Dumbarton Oaks proposals. Nor does the U.N. Charter contain any positive proposals for the protection of minorities, although it states that the protection of human rights should be "without distinction as to race, sex, language or religion" (Article 1, listing the purposes of the United Nations). True, the Preparatory Commission had proposed that the Commission on Human Rights (operating under the Economic and Social Council) should include the protection of minorities among its objectives, but it was not until March 1947 that, on the initiative of the Soviet Union, a Sub-Commission on Prevention of Discrimination and Protection of Minorities was created as a subordinate body of the Commission on Human Rights.

The purposes of the Sub-Commission (as it will be referred to from now on) were as follows:
to examine what provisions should be adopted in the definition

10

of the principles which are to be applied in the field of the prevention of discrimination on grounds of race, sex, language or religion, and in the field of the protection of minorities, and to make recommendations to the commission [on Human Rights] on urgent problems in these fields [and] to perform any other functions which may be entrusted to it by the Economic and Social Council or the Commission on Human Rights.16

These purposes in 1949 were downgraded to "undertake studies," so as to remove the implications that the Sub-Commission should concern itself with "urgent problems in these fields." The status of the Sub-Commission within the U.N. structure was also low; it could not communicate directly with member states, or even with the Secretary General, and only indirectly with the General Assembly. Even its parent body, the Commission on Human Rights tended to ignore it, and on several occasions the very existence of the Sub-Commission was in danger. Nor was the Economic and Social Council of much help, instead, it suspended the Sub-Commission - under the pretext of re-organization. Ultimately, it was the General Assembly which came to the rescue and requested the ECOSOC in 1952 to continue the Sub-Commission indefinitely.

From then on both the Economic and Social Council and the Commission on Human Rights started to take a more positive view of the Sub-Commission and its work.

One of the reasons for the lowly status of the Sub-commission, and for the low esteem of its work, was the priority given to two major concerns of the members: the prevention of genocide, and the protection of human rights in general. These two issues appeared to be of more importance and of more urgency, than any consideration of some new system of minority protection. As it turned out, however, the latter could not be totally separated from the former two. During the preparatory works of the Convention on the Prevention and Punishment of the Crime of Genocide, as well as those of the Universal Declaration of Human Rights, the question whether to include special provisions concerning minorities was hotly debated.

The Draft Convention, which served as a basis for the work of the Ad Hoc Committee on Genocide in the spring of

1948, defined the crime according to a three-fold classification: (1) physical genocide, that is, the destruction of groups by the physical destruction of individuals; (2) biological genocide, that is, the prevention of births within a group; (3) cultural genocide, "the brutal destruction of the specific characteristics of a group" by means designed to undermine its cultural and linguistic traditions.[17]

Opposition developed in the Ad Hoc Committee itself to the concept of "cultural genocide," and a clarification from the Secretariat pointed out that the will of the General Assembly, which initiated the project, was interpreted as calling for the definition of genocide with reference to "the actual destruction of a human group and not to restrictions, ill-treatment, or oppression of that group."[18] Despite opposition by France and the United States, the Ad Hoc Committee voted to retain the concept of cultural genocide in the draft convention; but subsequently the Sixth (Legal) Committee of the General Assembly reversed that decision and voted to delete the reference to cultural genocide. The fall 1948 session of the General Assembly went along with that; thus the United Nations passed up its first opportunity to support officially the concept of positive minority rights. Nevertheless, the Convention, adopted on December 9, 1948, still included the basic right of physical existence by declaring "acts with the intent to destroy, in whole or in part, a national, ethnical, racial or religious group as such" to be crimes under international law.[19]

Minority rights fared even worse in the Universal Declaration of Human Rights. Although the first draft produced by the Secretariat included an article calling for the right of minorities to use their own languages and to maintain schools and other cultural institutions, by the time of its final adoption all proposals for the recognition of positive minority rights had been deleted. Instead, the question was referred for further study to the Sub-Commission in the Human Rights Commission. All the Declaration contains in relation to minorities is the provision in Article 2: "Everyone is entitled to all the rights and freedoms set forth in this Declaration, without distinction of any kind, such as race, color, sex, language, religion, political or other opinion, national or social origin, property, birth or other status."[20]

It should be noted at this point that the Universal Declaration of Human Rights was simply a declaration which at best created a moral obligation for the members. The next step was to develop an international instrument that would create legal obligations on the part of its signatories. Eventually, the General Assembly (at its 6th Session) decided to divide the projected multilateral convention into two independent parts, a Covenant on Economic, Social, and Cultural Rights, and a Covenant on Civil and Political Rights. Both of these, debated for several years and redrafted a number of times, were finally adopted by the General Assembly on December 16, 1966, together with an Optional Protocol to the Covenant on Civil and Political Rights. Their adoption signified an important departure from previous practice; the Covenant on Civil and Political Rights, for the first time in the history of the United Nations, provides for the legal protection of minorities. Article 27 of the Covenant reads:

In those States in which ethnic, religious or linguistic minorities exist, persons belonging to such minorities shall not be denied the right, in community with the other members of their group, to enjoy their own culture, to profess and practise their own religion, and to use their own language.21

The United Nations and the Protection of the Rights of Minorities

The inclusion of Article 27 in the Covenant on Civil and Political Rights was an indication of growing concern for the protection of minorities both within the United Nations framework and within the international community at large. While the Paris Peace Treaties of 1947 stressed human rights in general terms, the Treaty concluded with Austria in 1955 already went farther and included provisions for the protection of the Slovene and Croat (but not any other) minorities.22 And even though at first the United Nations was reluctant to set up special minority rights' protection and preferred to subsume the minority problem under a general problem of human rights, minorities were not totally forgotten.

Already at its First Session, the General Assembly adopted a draft resolution, submitted by Egypt, calling upon governments "to put an immediate end to religious and so-called racial persecution and discrimination." The resolution was aimed at the allegedly oppressive treatment of certain minorities in Central Europe.23 In addition, the United Nations had dealt with the problems of certain minorities in specific cases: The Palestine Case in 1947, 1948, and 1949; and the Case of the Italian Colonies between the years 1948 and 1951.24

Additionally, as early as Dec. 14, 1960, the UNESCO Convention Against Discrimination in Education contained the following provision in Article 5, part 1:

The States Parties to this convention agree that . . . . (c) It is essential to recognize the right of members of national minorities to carry on their own educational activities, including the maintenance of schools and, depending on the educational policy of each State, the use or the teaching of their own language. . .25

The really significant departure from previous United Nations practice, however, occurred in the year 1971 when, after a number of preliminary studies, the Sub-Commission on Prevention of Discrimination and Protection of Minorities (with the approval of its parent body, the Commission on Human Rights) authorized the preparation of a major study concerning the problem of minorities and the possible protection of their rights. After six years of laborious investigation into the national and international legal position of minorities in the twentieth century, the study was completed in the summer of 1977 and was published as document E/CN .4/Sub.2/384 and Addenda 1-7, bearing the title: Study on the Rights of Persons Belonging to Ethnic, Religious and Linguistic Minorities, prepared by a well-known Italian jurist, Franceso Capotorti, Special Rapporteur. This long-awaited study (commonly known as the Capotorti Study) was sent out to all member nations of the U.N. and initiated a new chain of events.

In May, 1978, the Commission on Human rights in Geneva transmitted a number of documents dealing with minority rights to the governments of the member nations. One of the documents was a "Draft Declaration on the Rights of Persons Belonging to National, Ethnic, Religious and Linguistic Minorities," submitted by the government of Yugoslavia for discussion at the 34th Session of the Commission on Human

14

Rights in March, 1978. The Commission requested U.N. members to respond to the Yugoslav proposal and other related documents so that discussions on the subject in 1979 would have the benefit of a wide range of views. According to one scholar, the Commission's request "formally inaugurated global reconsideration of the problem of minorities, a matter which had been kept on an international backburner for most of the post-World War II period."26

Among Professor Capotorti's conclusions was a recommendation that the United Nations consider expanding the rights of minorities now only vaguely identified in Article 27 of the International Covenant on Civil and Political Rights. Governments, he argues, needed more detailed guidance in the application of general principles of minority protection. Evidently, the Commission on Human Rights agreed.

It will be years before we know whether the proposal for a declaration on minority rights has sufficient world-wide support to survive the cumbersome and politically charged procedures of the United Nations system. If it does, it will be only a first step toward creating eventually a more binding international convention. A number of governments have already transmitted their answer to the Commission. Non-governmental international organizations are also submitting proposals. Thus, for example, the Munich-based International Institute for Nationality Rights and Regionalism submitted two drafts: one for a universal Convention of the United Nations, the second for a European Regional Protocol for the protection of national or ethnic groups or minorities.27

Currently, the process of identifying and defining minority rights is attracting considerable attention from governments. "To some of them, troubled with civil strife and seccessionist claims, minority rights will inevitably appear seditious. To others, minority rights will seem to contradict and in some ways jeopardize progress in regard to general human rights. The manifest failure of the now defunct League system to prevent the manipulation and mistreatment of European minorities in the period between the two world wars will undoubtedly cause at least some statesmen to reflect on the wisdom of again assuming even modest international responsibility for safeguarding minority rights. But it will be difficult . . . for most statesmen to resist a nominal declaration and, ultimately even a binding convention on minority rights."28 After a rather long period of neglect, international momentum again seems to be on the side of minorities.

NOTES:

1. For the wording of this undertaking in the original French see C.A. Macartney, **National States and National Minorities**, 2nd. ed. (New York: Russell, 1968), P. 160.
2. Inis L. Claude, Jr., **National Minorities: An International Problem** (Cambridge: Harvard University Pr., 1955, p 1 2.
3. Alfred Cobban, The National State and National Self-Determination (London: Collins, 1969), p. 86
4. The text of Clemenceau's letter if reproduced in Oscar 1. Janowsky, **Nationalities and National Minorities** (New York: Macmillan, 1945), p 179-84.
5. A collection of these instruments is found in **League of Nations, Protection of Linguistic, Racial and Religious Minorities** by the League of Nations, 1927 I.B.2.
6. Claude, p. 17, referring to **The Public Papers of Woodrow Wilson**, 1, 463, 543.
7. See Pablo de Azcarate y Florez, **League of Nations and National Minorities** (New York: Carnegie Endowment, 1945), p. 82.
8. Claude, p. 19.
9. Andre Mandelstam, **La Protection des Minorites** (Paris: Hachette, 1925), p. 53-70.
10. Adatci's Report is reproduced in full in the Appendix to Pablo de Azcarate y Florez, **League of Nations and National Minorities** (New York: Carnegie Endowment, 1945). Azcarate was head of the League's Minority Section.
11. Claude, p. 30; and see his Chapter 3, "The Failure of the League Minority System." Detailed criticism is also offered by Macartney, Chapter 10, and by F. P. Walters, **A History of the League of Nations** (London: Oxford University Press, 1965), Chapter 34. The operating procedure is described in detail in the Adatci Report. A good legal analysis of the Minority Treaty obligations is found in Andre Mandelstam, **La Protection des Minorites**, (Paris: Hachette, 1925).
12. Macartney, p. 502.
13. Macartney, p. 505.
14. Quoted by Macartney, p. 506.
15. Macartney, pp. 506-507. This clause was not included in the Bulgarian Treaty because of Soviet opposition. Later, at the insistence of the U.S.A., Italy,

Yugoslavia and Czechoslovakia had to assume similar obligations.

16. United Nations Document, E/259, p.5
17. U.N. Document, E/447.
18. U.N. Document, E/AC25/3, p. 6.
19. See Articles I and II, in Walter Laqueur and Barry Rubin, **The Human Rights Reader** (Philadelphia: Temple University Press, 1979), p. 201-202
20. **Human Rights Reader**, p. 198. For a more detailed analysis of the drafting, debating, and adopting of the Genocide Convention and the Declaration of Human Rights see Chapter 12 in Claude, National Minorities.
21. Human Rights Reader, p. 224, Article 26 guarantees to all persons "equal and effective protection against discrimination on any ground such as race, color, sex, language, religion," . . . etc. Both Covenants also assert the right of self-determination. Neither of them contains provisions for effective enforcement in the event of its violation.
22. See Article 7 of the Peace Treaty signed by the Allied Powers and Austria on May 15, 1955, in Vienna.
23. **New York Times**, November 10 and 20, 1946.
24. See Claude, Chapter 13, "The United Nations and Specific Minority Problems." According to him "The United Nations displayed a rare willingness in the Eritrean case to involve itself in minority problems." p. 189.
25. Burns H. Weston, Richard A. Falk and Anthony A. D'Amato, **International Law and World Order** (St. Paul, Minn.: American Casebook Series, West Publishing Co., 1980), p. 541. Unfortunately subsections i, ii, and iii of Art. 5, par. I, sect. c., contain some restrictions on the exercise of this right.
26. Robert G. Wirsing, **Cultural Minorities; Is the World Ready to Protect Them?**, (Chapel Hill N.C.: Paper delivered at the Annual Conference of the International Studies Association, October 27-28, 1978), p. 1.
27. Felix Ermacora and Theodor Veiter, **Right of Nationalities and Protection of Minorities: Draft of an International Convention and of a European Protocol** (Munich: International Institute for Nationality Rights and Regionalism, 1978), Published In English, French, and German. The Draft Convention is now being co-sponsored by the London-based Minority Rights Group.
28. Wirsing, p.2.

II. CAN THE UNITED NATIONS PROTECT THE RIGHTS OF MINORITIES?

Discrimination against minorities, their persecution and elimination, sometimes through forced assimilation, sometimes through physical extermination, has been a perennial problem in human history. Books dealing with past history, and newspapers focusing on current events equally abound in examples. Indigenous minorities in the Americas; tribal minorities in Africa ;national and ethnic minorities in Europe; religious, linguistic, and ethnic minorities in the Middle East and elsewhere in Asia; there seems to be hardly a place on earth free of the plight of minorities.

Efforts by the international community to offer some orderly system of protection to minorities are relatively new, dating from the turn of the century. Historically, attempts to protect minorities against persecution took the form of occasional intervention by one or more states on behalf of their co-religionists in other countries. Later practice included guarantees of religious freedom for people of territories ceded to other countries either voluntarily, or under force. Where religious division was identical with national division, religious guarantees protected an entire nationality within a state.[1]

The first important international instrument to contain clauses safeguarding not only religious, but also national minorities, was the Final Act of the Congress of Vienna with regard to Polish nationals.[2] Later in the nineteenth century rights of ethnic and linguistic minorities were also given limited recognition. A more systematic protection of minorities emerged with the establishment of the League of Nations, but even this was limited in scope and applied only to some nations. Efforts to create a more comprehensive system of wider application within the framework of the United Nations did not begin until quite recently.3

Originally, the framers of the United Nations Charter assumed that by protecting the human rights of all persons, the rights of minorities would also be protected. Consequently, the Charter does not contain any proposal for the protection of minorities, although it states in Article 1 that the protection of human rights should be "without distinction as to race, sex, language or religion." The Universal Declaration of Human Rights, adopted in December 1948, did not go much farther either. The only provision which may be interpreted to refer to minorities is in Article 2: "Everyone is entitled to all the rights and freedoms set forth in this Declaration, without distinction of any kind, such as race, color, sex, language, religion, political or other opinion, national or social origin, property, birth or other status." More important, in this respect, with the Convention of the Prevention and Punishment of the Crime of Genocide, which included at least the basic right of physical existence for minorities, by declaring "acts committed with the intent to destroy in whole or in part, a national, ethnical, racial or religious group as such" to be crimes under international law.4

An important development was the inclusion of the following provision in Article 27 of the International Covenant on Civil and Political Rights:

In those States in which ethnic, religious or linguistic minorities exist, persons belonging to such minorities shall not be denied the right, in community with the other members of their own group, to enjoy their own culture, to profess and practise their own religion, and to use their own language.5

In addition, the United Nations Educational, Social and Cultural Organization Convention Against Discrimination in Education contains the following provision in Article 5, part 1: The States Parties to this Convention agree that . . . (c) It is essential to recognize the right of members of national minorities to carry on their own educational activities, including the maintenance of schools and, depending on the educational policy of each State, the use or the teaching of their own language . ..6

The first major break for minorities came in 1978, when Yugoslavia introduced a Draft Declaration for discussion at the meeting of the Commission on Human Rights. Yugoslavia, itself, is a country consisting of many different nationalities.

The way the Yugoslavs handle this problem, in a country where practically everybody is a national or ethnic minority, is by means of "ethnic federalism." That is, they created a federal republic consisting of a relatively small number of component parts as compared to the fifty states of the United States of America. Together, six ethnic republics and two autonomous provinces make up the Socialist Federal Republic of Yugoslavia. The Yugoslavs thought that their experience in granting certain rights to all minorities could be used somehow on an international level, so they introduced their proposal to the United Nations Human Rights Commission.

The Sub-Commission on the Prevention of Discrimination and Protection of Minorities authorized the preparation of a study, undertaken by an Italian jurist, Francesco Capotorti. He and his team of researchers worked for six years and produced and submitted a report on the worldwide problem of minorities. The Sub-Commission circulated the report to all member countries of the United Nations, suggesting that some action might be needed. Yugoslavia, after consultations with several other countries, initiated the action.

To observers it appeared that the draft declaration was received favorably, and there was discernible optimism concerning its eventual adoption. The Commission requested all United Nations members to respond to the Yugoslav proposal and other related documents so that discussions scheduled for the following year would have the benefit of a wide range of views. According to a minority rights scholar, the request of the Commission "formally inaugurated global reconsideration of the problem of minorities, a matter which had been kept on an international backburner for most of the post-World War II period."[7] The same scholar also observed that despite some anticipated difficulties, "it will be very difficult for most statesmen to resist a nominal declaration and, ultimately, even a binding convention on minority rights".[8]

The guarded optimism concerning the eventual passage of the draft declaration was based less on the initial reaction to it (only 26 countries sent in written comments during the first two years), than on the expectation that many United Nations members would consider such a declaration to be in their best interest. By taking timely action, political stability could be shored up or restored in some parts of the world where discontented minorities threatened the internal order and held out the possibility of foreign intervention or manipulation; territorial unity could be strengthened where a demand for self-determination may have raised the specter of secession; terrorism may be prevented or tempered. Support was expected "from fear that inaction will increase vulnerability to external subversion and internal fragmentation."9

Some critics, however, were skeptical from the very beginning, pointing out the dismal record of the United Nations in preventing states from discriminating, or even from committing genocide, against oppressed minorities. A well-known student of minority affairs explained that the passivity of the United Nations regarding the blatant, massive, and often violent methods of ethnic or racial discrimination by many of its member states was easy to understand:

Since the United Nations is in fact an organization of states (90 per cent of which are multi-national, and thus fear ethnic dissidence), it has not surprisingly taken a pro-state, anti-nation position on virtually every issue. Insistence by a member state that its ethnic policy is strictly an internal matter is generally sufficient for the United Nations to maintain a discreet silence over brutal misdeeds. The passivity of the United Nations on the issue of minority rights is further accentuated by the fact that its member states are represented in the United Nations by the very same elites that formulate and enforce discriminatory policies.10

A somewhat more than cursory look at the procedural aspects of adopting the draft declaration is rather enlightening, it closely reflects some of the substantive issues of minority protection: What is a minority? What rights are to be protected? Who shall enjoy those rights? Individuals only, or the group? Or perhaps both? How shall the protection of rights be implemented?

Initially, the Commission on Human Rights agreed to accept Capotorti's definition of a minority as a working definition, and created an open-ended working group to discuss the declaration and produce a text acceptable to all members.11

When the members of the working group met to rewrite the proposal, they began with the preamble, which is rather lengthy, and right there they ran into a problem. The title of the draft declaration originally referred to "The Rights of National, Ethnic, Religious, and Linguistic Minorities." This had to be changed to "Rights of Persons Belonging to . . . Minorities" at the request of countries who objected to the idea of conferring rights on minorities as groups. Only three countries out of the twenty-six, namely the German Democratic Republic, India, and Yugoslavia, indicated outright support for group rights. Nine countries supported the draft declaration fully, while ten suggested revision. Fourteen accepted the definition of the term minority, while eight suggested that there may be danger in that definition. And while nine countries indicated full support, and eleven partial support, only two countries (Greece and the Ivory Coast) registered no support for the draft declaration. There was, of course, the ominous silence of the majority: the lack of response from four-fifths of the United Nations member nations. Still, the working group decided to proceed with its task.

Next, some countries objected to the term "national minority". The term "national minority" is well known in Europe, but it is not known in Asia, Africa, or South America, where there they recognize only ethnic, religious, and linguistic minorities, creating an immediate objection. This objection was handled by an ingenious device of United Nations working groups, borrowed from parliamentary practice. They put the word "national" in square brackets indicating that when the entire declaration is rewritten or marked up, they will sit down again and decide whether or not the word "national" will be left in the text, or eliminated.

By 1982, the working group had come to the point where everyone agreed on the preamble. The following year they started to work on the first operative article. There were five operative articles in the original proposal; since then a sixth operative article has been added.12

When, in 1983, the working group sat down to tackle the operative articles of the draft declaration the difficulties continued. The sessions of the working group were not well attended, and those in attendance could not agree on a single article. The only agreement they reached was to try again in 1984. The next try almost ended in disaster for the draft declaration. When, after several futile attempts, the working group finally convened for a lengthy evening session (attended by half-a-dozen representatives of the member states, and the author of this paper), the fragile consensus that may have hitherto existed suddenly got unstuck. The representative from Senegal, a senior diplomat (other states were represented by junior members of their delegations), announced that his government did not find the definition of minority, contained in the Capotorti Study, satisfactory for continuing the deliberations on the draft declaration. He then suggested that the Sub-Commission on Prevention of Discrimination and Protection of Minorities be asked to produce a new definition, acceptable to all concerned, and that until this was accomplished the working group should suspend further consideration of the draft declaration. The day was saved by the compromise proposal of the representative of Greece, who suggested that the deliberations be continued even while the Sub-Commission was grappling with the problem of a definition.

On March 6, 1984, the members agreed that they would resume their work again in 1985 to consider a preliminary consolidated text of Article 1, which was to be prepared by the Chairman-Rapporteur, taking into consideration all the proposals and comments made thus far. Assistant Secretary General Kurt Herndl, Director of the Centre for Human Rights, in his closing speech of the 1984 session, identified some issues which he thought should be designated as high priority for the next year: one of these issues was "protecting the rights of minorities." He said this was an area which has been a fundamental issue since the establishment of the League of Nations. He concluded his report with an appeal to the members of the commission, "As the situation of millions of human beings is involved here, and as the issues are humanitarian in nature, it might be appropriate to renew efforts and to inject fresh impetus in this field."[13]

In March 1985, the members of the working group decided that until the Sub-Commission provided them with an acceptable definition they would not discuss the draft declaration at all. Actually, the Sub-Commission already considered the question of the definition in August 1984, when it met in Geneva for its 37th Session. In that meeting, the subject was dealt with in the following way: one of the members of the Sub-

Commission (allegedly the French member) suggested in the interests of time the Sub-Commission postpone the question of this definition until its 1985 session. Since there was no objection to this proposal, it was accepted, and that was how things stood in March 1985. The working group was waiting for the Sub-Commission to meet again in August 1985; and perhaps attempt the re-definition of the term minority. The working group's hand was strengthened by resolution 1985/53, in which the Commission urged the Sub-Commission to give highest priority, at its next session, to consideration of the proposals for the new definition of the term minority. Accordingly, the Sub-Commission, at its 38th session, considered a report prepared by one of its members, the Canadian Judge Jules Deschenes, and adopted resolution 1985/6 of August 28, 1985 (E/CN.4/Sub.2/1985/31 and Corr.1). It transmitted to the Commission Mr. Deschenes' study and proposal concerning a definition of the term minority, even though the Sub-Commission was unable to agree on it. The definition ran as follows:

"A group numerically smaller than the rest of the population of a State, in a non-dominant position, whose members - being citizens of the State - possess ethnic, religious or linguistic characteristics differing from those of others of the population and show, if only implicitly, a sense of solidarity directed towards preserving their culture, traditions, religion or language."

In addition, for the 42nd session of the Commission in 1986, the Delegation of Senegal also proposed a definition of the term minority in the following language:
"A 'minority' is a group of citizens of a State, or a separate community of individuals living in a numerical minority and in a non-dominant position in a specific country, locality or region, enjoying genuine homogeneity stemming from a race, a religion, a language or its own traditions and whose members are linked by a sentiment of solidarity and mutual assistance in order to perpetuate the values that characterize them and to co-exist peacefully on terms of de jure and de facto equality with the majority." (E/CN.4/1986/WG.5/WP.3)

In 1986, these two proposed definitions enabled the working group to proceed with the discussion of the draft declaration and tentatively to agree on the text of operative Article 1.

In their deliberations, members of the working group also were assisted by the written comments of those twelve countries which responded to a new request for comments on the draft declaration. Additional progress was made at the Commission's 43rd session in 1987, during which the working group reached a tentative agreement on the somewhat altered text of Article 2.

The fact, however, remains that most member nations are still reluctant to address themselves to the problem of minorities. And since the political will seems to be missing, it may take a long time before a declaration on the rights of minorities will be proclaimed by the United Nations.

Assuming that a declaration will be proclaimed eventually, it will be simply a declaration of principles, analogous in a sense to the Universal Declaration of Human Rights. Transforming these principles into a set of legally binding obligations in the form of an international covenant will be yet another hurdle to be tackled.

This may be the reason why, at this time, there are no plans or suggestions for the forms of implementation the rights of minorities should take.

How can one then evaluate this entire situation? What is the status of the international protection for the rights of minorities? As long as there is no agreement on who the minorities are, and what their rights are, the protection itself is left entirely to the individual countries. In some cases there are regional human rights forums, like the European Court of Human Rights. Also there are some political bodies like the Council of Europe and the European Parliament which are interested in the subject; but outside Europe there seems to be much less interest. Even in the United States there is not much interest. The official attitude of the United States government, and the representative of the United States in the Human Rights Commission, is a very cautious one. The United States, it seems, does not want to antagonize or appear in an adversary role with some of its allies who have minority problems. Senegal would be a good example; it is a country which is friendly toward the United States, and considered to be a democracy. Then there are countries like Brazil (which has problems with its indigenous minorities), India, Turkey, and others that are included in this category.

The difficulties facing the promotion of the rights of minorities on a world-wide basis are many. One of the difficulties is, as evidenced on the continent of Africa, the many linguistic, ethnic, and tribal minorities that alter the approach needed. The representative of Senegal said, "our main task as we see it is to build a nation, to forge a nation, a single nation out of the many tribal societies." What would be the logical continuation of this line of thinking? It could easily be: If there is an international instrument granting rights to minorities, then maybe some of those minorities would not want to merge into one nation and let themselves be molded into one national society.14

The problem of minorities is a world problem. It will not go away by sidetracking the issue of their protection on the basis that the term minority must be defined in a way acceptable to all concerned. Yet, this is exactly what happened in the 1950s and 1960s when the problem was referred to the Sub-Commission on Preventing of Discrimination and Protection of Minorities by the United Nations Commission on Human Rights. It is happening again today.

Assimilation, population transfer, or genocide are not acceptable answers, certainly not for the minorities concerned. Frontier revision could eliminate or reduce the scope of some minority problems, but the redrawing of borders is seldom done on a voluntary basis. Ethnic federalism, consociation, multiculturalism or multilingualism, all are considered as "defusing responses" to minority problems. However, they are unlikely to be employed in exactly those states where minorities suffer most.15 Other alternatives are called for, alternatives whose implementation does not depend on the whims of some majority bent on maintaining domination.

The task of designing a workable approach is a momentous one, and requires the collaboration of statesmen, diplomats, international lawyers, social scientists, and others. Many members of the international community already have come to recognize that pluralistic societies are here to stay and cultural differentiation by race, religion, language, and ethnicity is an existing fact in many nations, new or old. Now "we must close the gap between theories which accept group conflict, and the realities of modern nationhood that require groups to live together peacefully or else resort to destructive conflict." It is suggested that to take the first step toward the international protection of minorities, a theory of minority rights must be forged: one which recognizes minorities should have certain rights as groups and as individuals.

The basis for this is laid down already in Article 27 of the International Covenant on Civil and Political Rights, cited above. If it is accepted that the recognition of a problem is a prerequisite to its solution, then we should recognize that "the principle of equality must be envisaged in terms of collectivities as well as individuals."16 Members of the international community reluctant to follow the more enlightened approach of other nations could be educated and pressured to do so. This seems to be the purpose of the draft declaration now pending in the United Nations Commission on Human Rights, with its cautious language falling short of recognizing group rights for minorities.

At present, the granting of certain rights to minorities and the protection of these rights basically is a domestic matter in each country, dependent upon the political and legal structure of the country, the will of the government, and the will of the people. Today's international conventions and rules seek to give expression to standards which already exist in many countries and which have been deemed to serve as standards for the entire international community. Some such international standards for the treatment of minorities already exist today despite the lack of a comprehensive instrument. In addition, human rights standards also are applicable to minorities or individuals belonging to minorities. "But where such rules and standards are rejected or disregarded in a particular country, their enforcement from outside must be a kind of intervention which ranges from political influence to the use of coercion or force."17

Intervention, of course, is forbidden by the United Nations Charter. Yet, since its early days, objections raised by United Nations members to General Assembly or Security Council actions on the ground that they constituted intervention into domestic affairs have been always rejected by the majority if the issue was one of human rights. The reasoning was that the internationalization of human rights and freedoms made it no longer possible to regard them as purely domestic matters of a state.

It is on this basis that the United Nations, its organs, as well as other international governmental and non-governmental organizations, and indeed, the information media may intervene for the protection of minorities.18

Ineffective as these international "interventions" may seem to be, they constitute, for the time being, one of the most effective means for bringing pressure on governments. While hysterical and inaccurate denunciations which appear occasionally in the Western press do more harm than good, measured moral disapproval in the media of what is happening may also help. In this process non-governmental organizations could play a much more active part than has been the case until now. Unlike so many other issues, NGO-s have shown so far surprisingly little interest in the problem of minorities.

POST-SCRIPT

During the 45th Session of the U.N. Commission on Human Rights (February-March, 1989), the Open-ended Working Group on Minorities continued its slow-paced work on the Draft Declaration. Interest in the proceedings did not seem to have increased; of the 43 members of the Commission less than a dozen represented themselves in the discussions, mostly by junior members of their delegation. The thaw in U.S. - Soviet relations, however, made itself felt already. For the first time in the history of the Commission, a member of the "Socialist Bloc," namely Romania, was censured for persistent violations of human rights, including discrimination against minorities. The latter affected in particular the 2.5 million strong Hungarian minority, the largest national minority in Europe. The motion to appoint a Special Rapporteur to investigate the human rights situation in Romania passed by a comfortable majority, due to the fact that the Soviet Union and other "East Bloc" members decided not to participate in the voting, thereby substantially diminishing support for Romania.

Despite this and other signs of a Soviet - U.S.. rapprochement, the Working Group did not make much progress. This had to wait until the 46th (1990) Session, when both, interest and the pace of work picked up considerably, and a revised text of the Draft Declaration was adopted in "first reading." (See U.N. Doc. E/CN.4/1990/41, pages 11-14, attached.)

The "second reading" was to begin during the 47th Session in February, 1991, incentivated among others by a resolution from the U.N. General Assembly, urging the Commission to speed up work on the Draft Declaration. Indeed, in view of the increased ethnic conflict in Eastern Europe and many other parts of the world, the protection of the rights of minorities by the United Nations seemed to become ever more imperative.

Despite the increased feeling of urgency the Working Group made less headway than expected. By the end of the 47th Session only the Preamble and the first two operative paragraphs were approved in "second reading".

In view of this, at the suggestion of the Open-Ended Working Group, the Commission on Human Rights recommended that its parent body, the Economic and Social Council "authorize an open-ended working group to meet in an inter-sessional meeting complete its second reading of the draft declaration on the rights of persons belonging to national or ethnic, religious or linguistic minorities, with a view to submitting the text to the Commission at its forty-eighth session. This authorization was contained in Council resolution. 1991/30.

Subsequently the Working Group held 13 meetings during the period 2-13 December 1991. Delegations also held extensive informal consultations. Discussions proceeded rather smoothly, resulting in the approval of the remaining articles with some changes, and adding new ones.

At the 12th meeting, the Working Group considered the sequence in which the provisions adopted in second reading should appear in the final draft declaration. It decided to group certain provisions, to incorporate new articles or paragraphs adopted, and to renumber the operative part of the draft declaration accordingly. At the same meeting, the Working Group adopted the draft declaration as contained in Annex I of the Working Group's 16 December 1991 report, E/CN-4/1992/48, for submission to the 1992 session of the Commission.

The Commission. approved the draft declaration unanimously, and sent it on, through its parent body, to the U.N.General Assembly, which adopted it--also unanimously--on December 18, 1992, making it now a "Declaration." As such, it imposes moral and political, rather than legal obligations on the member states. In order to make it legally binding, the Declaration has to be transformed into a "Convention," a task that still lies ahead.

In the meantime the Commission has to grapple with the problem of how to make U.N. members abide by the principles and rights contained in the Declaration.

NOTES:

1. A brief historical account of the problem of protecting minorities may be found in United Nations Document E/CN.4/Sub.2/384, Rev. 1, bearing the title: **Study on the Rights of Persons Belonging to Ethnic, Religious and Linguistic Minorities**, commonly known as **The Caportorti Study**.

2. For the original French text of this undertaking see C. A. Macartney, **National States and National Minorities**, 2nd ed. (New York: Russell, 1968), p. 160. Macartney's book is an important contribution to the study of the problem of national minorities.

3. For a brief description and analysis of the League of Nations system of minority protection, see Edward Chaszar, "The Problem of National Minorities Before and After the Paris Peace Treaties of 1947." **Nationalities Papers**, Vol IX, No. 2 (Fall 1981), p.p. 195-206.

4. However, the hotly debated prohibition on cultural genocide ("the brutal destruction of the specific characteristics of a group" by means designed to undermine its cultural and linguistic traditions) was eliminated from the final text, adopted on December 9, 1948.

5. The Covenant was adopted by the United Nations General Assembly on December 16, 1966, together with an Optional Protocol. The United States did not accede to it until 1978, when President Carter signed it, pending a 2/3 approval by Senate -- still not given as of today.

6. This Convention was adopted on December 14, 1960. For the text see **Human Rights: A Compilation of International Instruments** (United Nations publication ST/HR/1/Rev. 2), pp. 33-36.

7. Robert G. Wirsing, "Cultural Minorities: Is the World Ready to Protect Them?" **Canadian Review of Studies in Nationalism**, Vol. VII, No. 2

(Fall 1980), p. 220. How and why the question of minority rights was kept on the backburner is excellently related in Inis L. Claude, Jr., **National Minorities: An Intentional Problem** (Cambridge: Harvard University Press, 1955).
8. Wirsing, p. 221.
9. Wirsing, p. 239.
10. Pierre L. van den Berghe, "Protection of Ethnic Minorities: A Critical Appraisal,"p. 346. In Robert G. Wirsing, editor, **Protection of Ethnic Minorities: Comparative Perspectives** (New York: Pergamon Press, 1981).
11. Capotorti used the following "interpretation" of the term minority: "for the purposes of the study, an ethnic, religious or linguistic minority is a group numerically smaller than the rest of the population of the State to which it belongs and possessing cultural, physical or historical characteristics, a religion or a language different from those of the rest of the population." Capotorti Study, p. 7. While this may certainly serve as a starting point for international action, it is far from being a generally accepted or acceptable definition. In fact, it may not be possible to find one.
12. The six operative articles are as follows:
Article 1
National, ethnic, linguistic and religious minorities (hereinafter referred to as minorities) have the rights to existence, to respect for and promotion of their own national, ethnic, linguistic, religious and other characteristics and to enjoyment of equality in relation to the rest of the population of the state in which they live.
Article 2
Any propaganda or other activity which is threatening or which may threaten the existence of minorities or discriminating against them or impeding their right to express and develop freely, on an equitable basis, their own characteristics is incompatible with the fundamental principles of the Charter of the United Nations and other relevant international instruments and should be prevented, condemned and proclaimed illegal by the member States of the United Nations.
Article 3
    1. Members of minorities shall enjoy all human rights and fundamental freedoms without any discrimination as to national or ethnic origins, language, religion or sex.
    2. For the purpose of realizing conditions of equality and comprehensive development of minorities, it is essential to create favorable conditions and to take measure which will enable them to freely express their characteristics and to develop their education, culture, language, traditions and customs and to participate on an equitable basis in the cultural, social, economic and political life of the country in which they live.
    3. Members of minorities should have the right to express and develop

cultural and other social links with people of their origin.
Article 4

1. The development of contacts and co-operation among States and the exchange of information and experience on the achievements and the realization of the rights of minorities in educational, cultural and other fields create favorable conditions for the promotion of the rights of minorities and for their general progress.

2. States members of the United Nations are invited to take the needs of minorities into account in developing their mutual co-operation, especially in the fields of education, culture and related areas of particular importance for minorities.
Article 5

1. In ensuring and promoting the rights of minorities, strict respect for the sovereignty, territorial integrity, political independence and non-interference in the internal affairs of these countries in which minorities live should be observed.

2. Respect for the aforementioned principles shall not prevent the fulfillment of the international commitments of States members of the United Nations in relation to minorities. Member States shall fulfill in good faith the commitment they have assumed under international treaties and agreements in which they are parties and under other international instruments.

3. The present Declaration shall not have the effect of diminishing the rights which minorities may enjoy by virtue of treaties or agreements concluded between two or more States, where such rights are not contrary to the letter and spirit of this Declaration.
Article 6
Member States of the United Nations shall endeavor, depending on their specific conditions, to create favorable political, educational, cultural and other conditions and to adopt adequate measures for the protection and promotion of the rights of minorities proclaimed in this Declaration.

For the entire proposed text, containing also the preamble, see United Nations document E/CN.4/Sub2/L.734. The text of that part of the Draft Declaration on which preliminary agreement has been reached so far is published as United Nations document E/CN.4/1 987/WG.5/CRP.1.

13. Personal notes from the 40th Session. The text of the speech is available from the Centre for Human Rights, Palais des Nations, Geneva.

14. The quotation is from personal notes. A remarkable study on this subject is that of a Nigerian scholar, Ladun Anise, "Ethnicity and National Integration in West Africa: Some Theoretical Considerations," in Raymond L. Hall (ed.), **Ethnic Autonomy-Comparative Dynamics: The Americas, Europe and the Developing World**. Pergamon Press, 1979.

15. These are discussed by Macartney, Claude Jr., and Van den Berghe, referred to earlier. See notes 2, 7, and 11.

16. Jay A. Sigler, Minority Rights: **A Comparative Analysis** (Westport:

32

Greenwood Press, 1983), p.194. Sigler presents a "provisional theory of minority rights," worthy of serious consideration.

17. **The International Protection of Minorities** (Minority Rights Group, Report No. 41, London, 1979), by James Fawcett, p. 4. This report contains a Draft Convention on the Protection of Minorities, presented by the Minority Rights Group to the United Nations Human Rights Commission. More comprehensive than the Yugoslav draft, it would also grant group rights to minorities. The question how the United States could contribute toward solving the international problem of minorities is ably discussed by Robert G. Wirsing's "The United States, and International Protection of Minorities," Chapter 9 in Natalie Kaufman Hevener (ed.), **The Dynamics of Human Rights in United States Foreign Policy** (New Brunswick, N. J.: Transaction Books, 1981). See in particular pp. 186-193.

18. On July 1st, 1983, Denmark, France, the Netherlands, Norway, and Sweden, each filed with the European Commission of Human Rights a complaint against Turkey for violations of the European Convention of Human Rights, of which Turkey is a signatory. While these were not in direct defense of the rights of minorities, they included many Kurds. Similarly, Amnesty International worked for the release of Kurds in Turkey charged with separatist activities, but not involved in violence. The human rights situation in Turkey was also considered in a closed session of the United Nations Human Rights Commission in February 1984, under its confidential procedure.

The Human Rights Commission dealt with the situation in Iran in public session. It has been doing so for the past three years, condemning Iran on each occasion for its gross and persistent violation of human rights, including the rights of Baha'is and other minorities. For a recent assessment of minority problems in the area see Edward Chaszar, "International Protection of Minorities in the Middle East: A Status Report," in **Middle East Review**, Vol. XVIII, No. 3 (Spring, 1986), pp. 37-48

III. International Protection of Minorities in the Middle East:

A Status Report*

*(This paper is an abbreviated form of a paper presented originally to the 18th Annual Duquesne History Forum,
Pittsburgh, November 1984.)

How does the lack of formal international instruments to protect the rights of minorities affect the situation of minorities in the Middle East? Do minorities enjoy any protection at all? To what extent and by whom? Can their situation be improved? How soon, and by what means?

In order to answer these questions, a brief survey of the Middle East minorities will be necessary.

For the purpose of this paper the Middle East is defined as the area of South-West Asia lying west of Afghanistan, Pakistan, and India. Thus defined it includes the Asian part of Turkey, Syria, Israel, Iraq, Iran, Jordan, Lebanon, and the countries of the Arabian peninsula (Kuwait, Bahrain, Qatar, Oman, United Arab Emirates, Southern Yemen, Yemen, and Saudi Arabia).1

National and ethnic minorities in the Middle East countries include the following. In Bahrain: Iranians, Indians, and Pakistanis. In Iran: Turkomans, Baluchis, Kurds, and Arabs. In Iraq: Kurds, Turks, and Palestinians. In Israel: Arabs (Palestinians) and a small number of Armenians. (The London-based Minority Rights Group, well-known among nongovernmental international organizations for its research and action concerning minority rights, considers Israel's Oriental Jewish immigrants also a minority.2 In Jordan: Palestinians, Kurds, and small minorities of Circassians and Armenians. In Kuwait: Iranians, Indians, Pakistanis, and Palestinians. In Lebanon: Armenians. In Oman: Baluchis, Indians, Iranians, and Africans. In Qatar: Indians, Iranians, and Pakistanis. In Saudi Arabia: immigrants from other Arab and Muslim countries, and Palestinians. In Syria: Kurds, Armenians, Turks, Circassians, Assyrians, and Palestinians. In Turkey: Greeks, Kurds and Armenians. In the United Arab Emirates: Iranians, Indians, and Pakistanis. In North Yemen: some Africans. In South Yemen: Indians and Somalis. (The ratio of these minorities relative to the total population of each country may be seen in Table 1 in the Appendix).

Religious minorities in these same countries are, depending on the country itself, Sunni Moslems or Shiite Moslems, Christians of all rites and denominations, Jews, Ismailis, Druzes, Yezides, Hindus and Baha'is (Table 2). Occasionally, a religious minority is at the same time an ethnic minority, or vice versa; take for example the Druzes, and the Armenians.

The situation of any and all of these national, ethnic, and religious minorities could be the subject of a separate study. Some of them have been studied, indeed, almost excessively, others hardly at all.3 In trying to come to grips with the problem of protecting minorities in the Middle East, a national minority, the Armenians; an ethnic minority, the Kurds; and a religious minority, the Baha'is, are selected here for closer scrutiny. The reason for these selections is that while practically all minorities have to suffer some kind of disadvantages or discrimination, these three have been outright persecuted and are, therefore, in dire need of some form of international protection.

THREE PERSECUTED MINORITIES

The Forgotten Genocide

At the time of the German invasion of Poland in 1939 Adolf Hitler supposedly declared:

"I have given orders to my Death Units to exterminate without mercy or pity men, women and children of the Polish-speaking race. It is only in this way that we can acquire the living room we need. After all, who today remembers the extermination of the Armenians?"4

The Armenians of the Middle East have perhaps the most tragic and least known history of any national, ethnic, or religious minority, particularly unknown in the Western Hemisphere.5 Today there are approximately 6 million Armenians spread all over the world, the majority of them living in the Soviet Union and in the Middle East. Historically, there is proof since 500 B.C. of an Armenian homeland, Great Armenia, comprising a large area of mountainous country, including most of eastern Anatolia (in today's Turkey), and much of present-day Kurdistan, stretching east as far as Persian Azerbaijan and the Soviet Karabagh, past Soviet Armenia. The latter today takes in only about ten per cent of ancient Great Armenia. Recent Turkish maps exclude all mention of Armenia; old Armenian place names are replaced and all mention of "Turkish Armenia" is prohibited.6

Like historic Poland, historic Armenia was also partitioned several times in the course of history, but it was not restored after World War I despite the promises of the Allied and Associated Powers, the United States included.

Speaking an Indo-European language, the Armenian people of old adopted Christianity early in the 4th Century A.D. Their language, their distinctive alphabet, and the establishment of a national Church proved vital in preserving Armenian national unity. Eventually, repeated rise and fall of the Armenian Kingdom lead to the "Great Dispersion" first in Asia Minor, then beyond. Adversities suffered under Byzantine rule were followed by those experienced under the Turks. During the Ottoman period Armenians were organized into their own millet, or semi-autonomous community, known until the fatal troubles of the nineteenth century as the "loyal Millet." Adversity in Persia - such as the deportations under Shah Abbas the Great in the 17th Century - prompted the spreading of the Armenians eastward, into India and beyond.

What is referred to in Armenian history as "The Era of Massacres" began late in the 19th Century. As the MRG Report put it:

In the course of a quarter of a century - between 1895 and 1920 - the Armenian race lost a million and a half persons by the gun or the bayonet, by deliberate starvation, and by privation and pestilence. About a third of all Armenians in the

36

world died a gruesome, painful death. This national catastrophe is comparable to that suffered by the Jews under the Hitler regime. No Armenian household today . . . is free of memories of this holocaust.7

The gruesome story of these massacres, started during the reign of Ottoman Sultan Abdul Hamid II, then continued and completed by the Young Turks and the new government, will not be retold here. Nor shall we dwell here on the broken promises of the Great Powers to restore an independent Armenia after World War I. The deal struck between Lenin and Kemal Ataturk eventually crushed all hopes for that solution; the only Armenia today is the Armenian Republic inside the Soviet Union.

Figures may be debated, facts may be denied or explained away - as they are in present-day Turkey - but the evidence of eyewitness accounts is overwhelmingly conclusive: The Armenian Holocaust did happen, and any self-respecting historian will say so. Moreover, this "genocide" is not forgotten; it is still a live issue, and appears to remain so for many years to come.

The number of Armenians in the Middle East today is estimated at 800,000. Of these, approximately 150,000 live in Syria, 180,000 in Lebanon, 200,000 in Iran, and 250,000 in Turkey. The figure for Turkey seems to be inflated, and probably includes many Armenians who changed their name and converted to Islam to avoid persecution. There are also Armenian communities in Iraq, Jordan, Israel (and if included in the Middle East, in Cyprus and Egypt).8

Lebanon may now be considered an Armenian disaster area (and the same would be true for Cyprus). Serious problems of a different nature beset the Armenians living in the authoritarian regimes of Syria, Iraq, an even more so in Iran. Finally, those in Turkey are discriminated against in many different ways.

Armenians living outside the Middle East and the Soviet Union are well organized, and they lobby through national governments and international organizations to press certain claims. Among others, they demand that the crime of Genocide committed against the Armenian nation in the 20th Century be condemned by the international community, preferably through the United Nations, and by Turkey. They demand that Armenians be permitted to return to their homeland; and, to end the injustice done to them, that the larger part of their homeland, now under Turkish occupation (and emptied of its original population), be returned to its rightful owners, the Armenians.

In fact, there is no unanimity among Armenians themselves how best to attain these goals. A desperate, militant minority favors violent action to keep the issue alive. This includes occasional acts of terrorism and "revenge" against innocent Turks who bear no responsibility for the terrible happenings of the past. It is doubtful whether acts of this nature help or hinder the Armenian cause. But, be it as it may, in view of their tragic history and unfortunate situation at present, it is reasonable to advocate some form of protection by the international community for the Armenian minority living today in the Middle East.[9]

The Fighting Kurds

Unlike the Armenians, who have been decimated, dispersed, forced into submission or made to accept reluctantly the precarious existence of minorities, the more numerous Kurds continue to fight for an independent (or at least autonomous) homeland in the Middle East. That homeland, however, lies today in five different independent countries, mainly in Turkey, Iraq, and Iran, with enclaves in Syria and the Soviet Union.

Kurdistan is not an independent state, but a "geographic expression," used in two different ways. Most maps mark Kurdistan as a mountainous region extending from south-east Turkey across the northernmost areas of Iraq into Iran's mid-western region. But some Kurdish sources claim as Kurdistan an area twice that size: the land stretching from the Taurus Mountains in the west to the Iranian plateau in the east, and from Mount Ararat in the north to the plains of Mesopotamia in the south. It also spills over into Soviet Armenia and Azerbaijan, thus equalling the area of France. (The fact that there is an administrative province in Iran named Kordestan - with predominantly Kurdish population - further complicates the matter of nomenclature.) This whole area is believed to be rich in natural resources.10

While there is disagreement over the size or location of Kurdistan, there seems to be total confusion concerning the number of Kurds. Census information is either woefully inadequate, or not published at all. In addition, governments opposed to Kurdish nationalism underestimate their numbers deliberately, while Kurdish nationalists exaggerate them. Minimum and maximum estimates of the Kurdish populations in the five countries where they reside are as follows.11

Country	Minimum	Maximum	Population Total
Turkey	3,200,000	8,000,00	35,666,500
Iran	1,800,000	5,000,000	28,448,000
Iraq	1,550,000	2,500,000	9,498,000
Syria	320,000	600,000	6,294,000
USSR*	80,000	300,000	13,132,000
Lebanon	40,000	70,000	2,645,000
Total:	6,990,000	16,470,000	

(*Armenia, Georgia, Azerbaijan)

The Kurds consider themselves the descendants of the ancient Medes, who were later conquered by - and supposedly fused with - the Persians in the 6th Century B.C. Their language is Indo-European, closely related to Persian, but the Kurds assert that they have a distinct and independent nationality. Certainly, they have no ethnic relationship with the Turks or the Arabs. As for religion, most of them are Muslims, belonging to the Sunni sect except in Iraq and Iran, where some Kurds are Shi'a Muslims. A few are Christians and Zoroastrians.

Much of Kurdish life still revolves around the tribe; the majority of Kurds are peasants, their lives controlled by the aghas, who are best likened to feudal landowners. Land distribution is still grossly unequal, although some improvements were made during the last twenty years through land reform. Overall, the economic, educational, and health condition of all Kurdistan is reported to be lamentable, "but this must be seen in the context of deprived conditions throughout many parts of the Middle East."12

Historically, the Kurds never enjoyed political

independence, but nationalism has been a recurring theme of Kurdish politics and literature throughout the centuries of their subjection. In the break-up of the Ottoman Empire after World War I, the Kurds had the prospect of independence under the Treaty of Sevres (1920) but, due mainly to the rise of Kemal Ataturk, the treaty was never put into effect. After his brutal suppression of the Armenian Republic, Kemal Ataturk crushed the Kurdish revolt and ended the hopes of an independent Kurdistan. The 1923 Treaty of Lausanne made no mention of either Armenia or Kurdistan.

Unfortunately for them, the Kurds may be one nation, but their nationalist movements in each country have functioned very much independently of each other. Thus, in the early 1970's it was only in Iraq that the Kurds called for "autonomy". The offer they received from the government was rejected as inadequate by their leader, the legendary General Barzani; and the deal struck between the Shah of Iran and President Hussein of Iraq the following year at the Algiers Conference sealed the fate of the Kurds. Without help from Iran their forces were to suffer defeat. Some 250,000 Kurds fled across the border to Iran. By the time government forces crushed Barzani's army, an estimated 600,000 to 750,000 persons were displaced. As an aftermath, 300,000 Kurds have been forcibly transferred southward to desert regions.[13]

Adversity befell the Kurds of Iran a few years later, following the Revolution of 1979. It was now the turn of the Kurds in Iran to rebel and fight for autonomy against overwhelming odds. Renewed fighting, year after year, met with defeat rather than success. The Islamic Republic of Ayatullah Khumayni opposes any move for Kurdish autonomy in Iran. For if the Kurds get their autonomy, what about the Turkomans, Baluchis, Azeris, and the Iranian Arabs? Iran is, after all, a country of many minorities.

Headlines in the newspapers from 1979 to 1982 tell the rest of the story. Today one finds only small news items announcing the imprisonment or execution of Kurdish "rebels" or "leftists" in Iran.[14]

The Kurds in Turkey are the most numerous, but possibly also the most oppressed. The 1965 Turkish census put their number as low as 2,180,000 according to mother tongue.

The true figure is thought to be well above five million, but Turkish authorities have tended to deny that the Kurds have a separate ethnic identity. ("They are not Kurds, but 'Mountain Turks'.") Prime Minister Nihat Erim even denied the existence of the Kurdish language, asserting that it was a mixture of Persian, Turkish and Arabic languages, with only 3,000 complete Kurdish words. He also expressed, in May 1971, the official attitude toward the Kurds in one of his speeches:

We accept no other nation as living in Turkey, only the Turks. As we see it, there is only one nation in Turkey: the Turkish nation. All citizens living in different parts of the country are content to be Turkish.[15]

A law passed in 1924 made it punishable to publish in Kurdish or to teach Kurdish in schools. Leaders of an organization to preserve Kurdish culture were prosecuted during the 1971-73 military dictatorship for "separatist activities," and the organization was banned. Thirty-six Kurdish intellectuals received jail sentences for being affiliated with the Kurdish Democratic Party. This was done under the Political Parties Act of 1964, which bans parties based on race or language other than Turkish

Whenever Kurdish discontent takes the form of violent opposition, the Turkish answer is martial law, severe repression, and deportation of Kurds. The insurrections of 1925 and 1930, and local risings in 1960 and 1970, or later, were all crushed.

This is the same Turkey which agreed in the Treaty of Lausanne to respect the rights of minorities; which is a signatory of the European Convention on Human Rights; and which has references in its Constitution to human rights, freedom of thought and freedom of expression. Of course, the Constitution forbids any activity considered harmful to the "national unity and the territorial integrity of the Turkish Republic." (Article 57). This is used to prosecute people accused of "separatist activities." As recently as September 1984 a number of people in Turkey were sentenced - and some executed - for "separatist activities," a term usually reserved for Kurds.[16]

The only recent change in the adverse relationship which exists between the Kurds and the governments of Iran, Iraq, and Turkey has been reported from Iraq. Due to the internal situation which developed there as a result of the Iraq-Iran war, the government again appears to be seeking an accommodation with the Kurds. In January, 1984, it was reported by diplomats that the Iraqi government "signed an agreement with Kurdish rebel leader Jalal Talabani for cease-fire in the Kurdish region and for 'free and democratic elections' to Kurdish legislative and executive councils." Supposedly the Government also agreed to allocate 30 percent of the budget to rehabilitate Kurdish areas devastated in the war with Iran and to finance development projects in the region. It remains to be seen whether this agreement will be implemented.[17]

The Persecuted Baha'is

Of all the religious minorities in the Middle East the plight of Iran's Baha'is is the saddest and commands most attention in world public opinion.

The Baha'i faith was originally an off-shoot of the Shi'a branch of Islam. It arose in Iran during the 19th century. The central figure (there were others) in the founding of Baha'ism, Baha'ullah, gradually dissolved the ties with Islam and developed the new faith into a separate religion.

Like all Muslims, Baha'is do not separate secular and spiritual affairs, not in theory anyway, and therefore Baha'ism could be described as a theocracy without priests. Baha'is regard their administrative system as a model for world government, which can be implemented gradually through peaceful means. Their peaceful approach is supported by the fact that they are forbidden to join political parties or secret societies, and at the same time they are to respect and obey the legal authority of the country where they live. They also believe in the equality of the sexes, racial harmony, universal education, and they abstain from alcohol.

Although official membership figures have not been published, estimates for the Baha'i world-wide community run from 1.5 to over 3 million, and for Iran between 150,000 to 350,000.[18]

To understand the attitude of Iranians toward Baha'ism requires some knowledge of Islamic history and dogma. Briefly stated, there is no universally accepted source of orthodoxy in Islam, and therefore it is difficult to define heresy, "but the nearest equivalent is bid'a, literally innovation, and there is no doubt among Muslims, both Shi'is and Sunnis, that the claims to prophethood by the Bab and Baha'ullah put them and their followers beyond the pale of Islam." 19 In Iran their religion is not considered a religion, and they cannot claim the protection they might otherwise expect as a religious minority. Jews, Christians, and Zoroastrians in Iran are accorded a second-rate, but safe status by the present Constitution, with certain limitations imposed on their religious and social practices. Baha'is are denied this status. They are "heretics" whose blood may be shed with impunity.20

In addition to religious prejudice and theological disapproval, Baha'is are also accused on political and moral grounds. The most serious among the political charges is that they cooperated with the Shah's regime. They are also accused of being agents of Zionism and imperialism; and because their marriage ceremony has never been recognized in Iran, Baha'i couples are considered to be living "in sin," and their children illegitimate. Charges of immorality also arise from the practice that sexes are not segregated at gatherings, as they are in Muslim ceremonies.

All these accusations can be refuted easily, because they are based on misunderstandings, oversimplifications, or malicious misinterpretations. Unfortunately, prejudice against the Baha'is in Iran is so deeply ingrained that all refutations are put down simply as "Baha'i propaganda."

The persecution of Baha'is in Iran has a long history, dating back to 1845. After some ups and downs one of the worst outbreaks occurred in 1955. Pressure of world public opinion, of many governments, and the United Nations proved effective in ending that wave of repression in which the mobs and the government collaborated, but not before a lot of damage had been done. The damage was not only material, but also psychological, especially in reviving prejudices. Dormant anti-Baha'i feeling was resuscitated in the younger generation.

Baha'is did not fare too well under the Shah's regime; there was considerable discrimination. But all the harassment they were subjected to was nothing compared to what happened since the 1979 Revolution. During the last five years Iran has been in gross violation of the human rights of its Baha'i citizens. The evidence that not only anti-'Baha'i fanatics, but also the Government are guilty appears to be overwhelming. Attacks on the Baha'i leadership, economic persecution, political and administrative persecution are well documents. According to U.S. government sources, since the Revolution more than 170 Baha'is have been executed or have died under torture in prison; many others have simply disappeared and are presumed dead. Today, more than 750 Baha'is are imprisoned, over 30 of them awaiting execution. The torturing of prisoners is common.21

International reaction to the persecution of Baha'is in Iran has been strong. Numerous international and national bodies have passed resolutions, often in strong terms, calling on the Iranian government to end human rights violations, including those of -- but not confined to -- the Baha'is. Accusations, however, are either met by a blanket denial, or are explained away.

A major study concerning the problem of minorities in the Middle East would have dealt with many more situations than the three selected here. It would have to address, first of all, the problem of the Palestinians (Arabs) in Israel, a problem of such magnitude that in the United Nations and elsewhere it is considered as a separate problem. Lebanon would also merit special consideration, for it is considered by many as a country inhabited entirely by minorities. In a sense this is true:

"There is not a single resident in Lebanon who cannot, in one sense or another, truthfully claim to belong to a minority. It is the conflicting aspirations and fears of these different [minority] components of Lebanese society confined in a small and rapidly urbanizing area, which lie at the heart of the continuing crisis in Lebanon today."22

Attention would have to be paid also to minorities as the Turkomans, Baluchis, and other small ethnic minorities; to religious minorities, as the Druzes or Christians, including the Copts of Egypt, if that country is added to the Middle East. Likewise, the inclusion of Cyprus would necessitate an examination of the Turkish minority there. In fact, good studies exist on most of these.23

Nevertheless, even the present study which is restricted to .

44

Armenians, Kurds, and Baha'is is sufficient to prove that a serious need exists in the Middle East for the international protection of minorities. In conclusion, let us examine therefore whether the rights of Middle East minorities can be protected, and if so, by what means?

THE PROTECTION OF MINORITIES RECONSIDERED

The problem of minorities is a world problem. The world will not make it disappear by sidetracking the issue of their protection on the basis that the term "minority" must be defined in a way acceptable to all concerned. Yet, this is exactly what happened in the 1950s and 1960s when the problem was referred to the Sub-Commission on Prevention of Discrimination and Protection of Minorities by the U.N. Commission on Human Rights. It is happening again today.

Assimilation, population transfer, or genocide are not acceptable solutions, certainly not for the minorities concerned. Frontier revision could eliminate or reduce the scope of some minority problems, but the redrawing of borders is seldom done voluntarily. Ethnic federalism, consociation, multiculturalism, or multilingualism are all considered as "defusing responses" to minority problems, but they are unlikely to be employed in exactly those states where minorities suffer most.24 Other alternatives are called for, alternatives the implementation of which does not depend on the whims of some majority bent on maintaining domination.

The task of designing a workable approach is a momentous one, and requires the collaboration of statesmen, diplomats, international lawyers, social scientists, and others. Many members of the international community have already come to recognize that pluralistic societies are here to stay, and cultural differentiation by race, religion, language, and ethnicity is an existing fact in many old as well as new nations. Now "we must close the gap between theories which accept group conflict, and the realities of modern nationhood that require groups to live together peacefully or else resort to destructive conflict."25 It is suggested that to take the first step toward the international protection of minorities, a theory of minority rights has to be forged, one which recognizes that minorities should have certain rights as groups, and not only as individuals. The basis for this has already been laid down in Article 27 of the International Covenant on Civil and Political Rights, cited above. If it is accepted that the recognition of a problem is a prerequisite to its solution, then we should recognize that "the principle of equality must be envisaged in terms of collectivities as well as individuals."26 Members of the international community reluctant to follow the more enlightened approach of other nations could be educated and pressured to do so. This seems to be the purpose of the Draft Declaration now pending in the U.N. Commission on Human Rights, its cautious language falling short of recognizing group rights for minorities.

The granting of certain rights to minorities and the protection of these rights is basically a domestic matter in each country, depending on the political and legal structure of that country, and on the will of the government and the people. Today's international conventions and rules merely give expression to standards which already exist in many countries and which have been deemed to serve as standards for the entire international community. Some such standards for the treatment of minorities already exist today despite the lack of a comprehensive instrument.

(These were referred to in the first part of this study.) In addition, human rights standards are also applicable to minorities or individuals belonging to minorities. "But where such rules and standards are rejected or disregarded in a particular country, their enforcement from outside must be a kind of intervention which ranges from political influence to the use of coercion or force."27

Intervention, of course, is forbidden by the United Nations Charter. Yet, since its early days objections raised by U.N. members to General Assembly or Security Council actions on the ground that they constituted intervention into domestic affairs have been always rejected by the majority if the issue was one of human rights. The reasoning was that the internationalization of human rights and freedoms made it no longer possible to regard them as purely domestic matters of a State.

It is on this basis that the United Nations, its organs, as well as other international governmental and non-governmental organizations, and indeed, the information media may intervene for the protection of Middle East minorities. On July 1st, 1983, Denmark, France, the Netherlands, Norway, and Sweden each filed with the European Commission of Human Rights a complaint against Turkey for violations of the European convention of Human Rights, of which Turkey is a signatory. While these were not in direct defense of the rights of minorities, they included many Kurds. Similarly, Amnesty International worked for the release of Kurds in Turkey charged with separatist activities, but not involved in violence. The human rights situation in Turkey was also considered in a closed session of the U.N. Human Rights Commission in February, 1984, under its confidential procedure.

The Human Rights commission dealt with the situation in Iran in public session. It has been doing so for the past three years, condemning Iran on each occasion for its gross and persistent violation of human rights, including the rights of Baha'is and other minorities. So far Iran has shrugged off all such "interventions," and does not cooperate with the Human Rights Commission in allowing on-the-spot investigation, or comply with the request to submit a report. Earlier, in July 1982, the Human Rights Committee (created by and for the signatory States of the International Covenant on Civil and Political Rights) heard a report by Iran on its implementation of the Covenant. The question raised by members of the Committee concerning specific violations of human rights, such as summary executions, torture, arbitrary arrest and detention, and denial religious freedom (particularly the repression of the Baha'is) were not answered satisfactorily. However, a promise was made that a detailed report would be submitted later.

Iraq has ratified the International Covenant on Civil and Political Rights in 1971, but it has not permitted international investigations of alleged human rights violations. Yet, violations are reported frequently and are subject to criticism and condemnation by individual speakers in meetings of the Human Rights Commission. The Government of Iraq does not reply to specific charges raised by non-governmental organizations, such as Amnesty International.

Ineffective as these international "interventions" may seem to be, they constitute for the time being one of the most effective means for bringing pressure on governments. Groups concerned with discrimination against minorities (and the Baha'is themselves in Iran) believe that the right kinds of collective protest can help. While hysterical and inaccurate denunciations which appear occasionally in the Western press do more harm than good, measured moral disapproval in the media of what is happening may also help. This seems to be particularly true with regard to Iran which is seeking to end its near isolation from the international community and win sympathy over the Iraqi invasion. As any diplomat would say, there are three ingredients for success: understanding for the opposite point of view, moderation, and patience.

NOTES:

1. **The New Columbia Encyclopedia** (Columbia University Press, 1975) also includes Egypt and Libya; **The Encyclopedia Americana** (Grolier, 1983) adds European Turkey, Cyprus, and the Sudan. The term is also used sometimes in a cultural sense "to mean the group of lands in that part of the world predominantly Islamic in culture, thus including the remaining states of N.Africa as well as Afghanistan and Pakistan." New Columbia Enc.; p. 1771. Governmental and Non-Governmental International Organizations, which deal with human rights issues, do not include North African countries in the term Middle East; this is the reason for my "narrow" definition.
2. Alfred Friendly, **Israel's Oriental Immigrants and Druses**. Minority Rights Group (London):Report No. 12 (1972).
3. On-line computer data search in the MIDEAST File (one of three M.F. data-banks
accessible in the IUP Library) offers ample proof of these generalizations. The number of articles dealing with minorities (as listed between January 1980 and September 1984) breaks down as follows: Jews, 1,022. Christians, 504. Kurds, 265. Maronites, 171. Indians, 109. Armenians, 103. Druzes, 45. Baha'is, 14. Ismailis, 12. Baluchis, 12. Circassians, 3. Turkomans, 3. Hindus, 2. Yazidi (Yezides), 0.
4. Quoted in **The Armenians**, Report No. 32 of the Minority Rights Group (London), New Revised Edition, 1978, p. 2, David Marshall Long and Cristopher J. Walker, joint authors. In my survey I relied heavily on the excellent reports of the MRG on the Armenians, the Kurds, Baha'is,
and others.

5.   A survey of students in my own World Politics classes produced the following results: Of the 96 students surveyed 37 said they had never heard of the Armenians. Of the remaining 59 only 33 knew that Armenians come from the Middle East, and only 18 of them had ever heard of the massacres or genocide commited against them. On the other hand, 36 identified Armenians with terrorism.

6.   According to the revised **Encyclopedia of Islam** Great Armenia (the Arminiyya of the Arab Abbasid geographers) takes in all the land between longitudes 37 and 49 East, and latitudes 37.5 and 41.5 North, a total area of approximately 115,000 square miles or 300,000 square kilometers. Reference in **The Armenians**, p.3. The latter also contains figures pertaining to the present distribution of Armenians in the world.

7.   **The Armenians**, p.5. Compare this figure, however, with that of Leo Kuper (800,000 plus) in **International Action Against Genocide** in Report No.53 of the Minority Rights Group (London,1982). Both **The Armenians** and Kuper's Report contain a brief historical account of the massacres, and list a number of sources. For a recent detailed historical study see Justin McCarthy, **Muslims and Minorities: The Population of Ottoman Anatolia and the End of the Empire** (New York University Press, 1983). His casuality figure of 600,000 is considered too low by some critics.

8.   **The Armenians**, p. 4.

9.   The restrictions on the various Armenian communities in the Middle East, and especially in Turkey, are described in the MRG Report cited. The report also points out that since World War II it has suited U.S. interests to "keep Turkey's eastern provinces empty and desolate as a 'buffer zone', rather than see them repopulated with Armenians on friendly terms with their brethren in the Armenian S.S.R. (p.2.) The **Country Reports on Human Rights Practices for 1983**, prepared by the U.S.Department of State (Washington: U.S. Government Printing Office, 1984) makes mention of complaints among minority religious groups in Turkey, without particular reference to the Armenian Church. See pp. 1115-1116.

10. **The Kurds**, Minority Rights Group Report No. 23, Third Edition, by Martin Short and Anthony McDermott (London, 1977), p. 5. R. D. McLaurin (ed.), **The Political Role of Minority Groups in the Middle East** (New York: Praeger, 1979) also contains an interesting chapter by William E. Hazen, "Minorities in Revolt: The Kurds of Iran, Iraq, Syria and Turkey," supplementing in a way the MRG Report. The book as a whole contributes substantially to an understanding of the Middle East minorities' problem. It also contains detailed population data on selected countries, showing religious, ethnic, linguistic, and national minorities (in that order).

11. **The Kurds**, p. 6. The figures are ten to twelve years old.

12. **The Kurds**, p. 7.

13. **The Kurds**, pp. 21 and 24. But the U.N. reported only 300,000 displaced

persons, and the Iraqi Ministry of Information admitted the resettlement of only between 30,000 and 40,000 Kurds.

14.   **Deadline Data on World Affairs** (Santa Barbara: ABC-Clio, Inc., 1984) index lists the following entries for Iran under "Minorities" since 1979: Kurdish Rebellion Seeks Autonomy, 1979 March 19; Attack on Kurd Leftists, 1979 April 20; Kurds Fight for Autonomy, 1979 July 1; Kurdish Revolt, 1979 August 13; Violence and Continuing Tension Between Ethnic Minorities and Government, 1980 January 7; Kurds Battle Revolutionary Guards, 1980 January 30; Kurdish Uprising Suppressed, 1980 October 14; Battles with Kurds, 1981 February 2; Iranian Forces' Assault Against Kurds, 1982 April 16; Kurdish Insurgence, 1982 October 17.

15.   **The Kurds**, p. 9.

16.   **The New York Times**, April 18, 1984, and October 15, 1984. Hundreds of Kurds were tried and sentenced also in 1983. See Amnesty International Report 1983, p. 281. For general restrictions on Kurds see the State Department's **Country Reports for 1983**. Pp.1118-19. According to the **Country Reports for 1982**, p. 1117, Kurdish language publications are still forbidden.

17.   **Deadline Data on World Affairs**, Iraq, 1984 January 3.

18.   The various publications from which I gleaned the facts about the Baha'is, offer widely different estimates. See MRG Report No. 51, **The Baha'is of Iran** (London 1982), by Roger Cooper,. p. 7; **Religious Persecution of the Baha'is in Iran**, Hearing Before the Subcommittee on Human Rights and International Organizations of the Committee on Foreign Affairs, House of Representatives, 98th Congress, 2nd Session, May 2, 1984 (Washington: U.S.Govt. Printing Office), p. 15; and "Plight of Iranian Baha'is," in Gist (U.S.Dept. of State, Bureau of Public Affairs), October 1984, p. 1.

19.   **The Baha'is of Iran**, p. 9.

20.   Ibid

21.   Gist, cited above, footnote 18 (p. 2). See also the State Department **Country Reports for 1983**, pp. 1141-43, and **Amnesty International Report 1983**, pp. 305 and 308.

22.   Lebanon: **A Conflict of Minorities**. Minority Rights Group Report No. 61 (London, 1983), by David McDowall, p. 7. See also **The Palestinians**, MRG Report No. 24, 3rd edition (London, 1979).

23.   A good study is Robert Brenton Betts, **Christians in the Arab East**, revised edition (Atlanta: John Knox Press, 1978). The Minority Rights Group has published reports on Cyprus (No. 30, 1976), and on Israel's oriental immigrants and Druzes, cited above in footnote 14. Valuable contributions to the problems of Middle East minorities may be also found in works of a more general nature: Jacob M. Landau, ed., **Man, State and Society in the Contemporary Middle East** (New York: Praeger, 1972) contains a chapter on "Religious and Ethnic Groups" by Gabriel Baer, and one on " Minorities in the Arab Orient Today" by Pierre Rondot. Dale F. Eickelman, **The Middle**

East: An Anthropological Approach (Englewood Cliffs: Prentice-Hall, 1981), pp. 157-174, writes about "Ethnicity and Cultural Identity." John Obert Voll, **Islam: Continuity and Change in the Modern World** (Boulder, Col.:Westview Press, 1982), pp. 268-271, offers brief comments on "Muslim Minorities in the Middle East," while William R. Polk's **The Arab World** (Cambridge: Harvard University Press, 1980) contains a brief chapter on "The Palestine Arab Diaspora." As mentioned before, some of these subjects, especially the Palestinians, Cyprus, and Lebanon, have a prolific literature, while others are rather neglected.

24. These are discussed by C. A. Macartney, **National States and National Minorities**, 2nd ed. (New York: Russell, 1968); Inis L. Claude, Jr., **National Minorities: An International Problem** (Cambridge: Harvard University Press, 1955); and Pierre L. Van den Berghe, "Protection of Ethnic Minorities: A Critical Appraisal," in Robert G. Wirsing, editor, **Protection of Ethnic Minorities: Comparative Perspectives** (New York: Pergamon Press, 1981).

25. Jay A. Sigler, **Minority Rights: A Comparative Analysis** (Westport: Greenwood Press, 1983) p. 194. Sigler presents a "provisional theory of minority rights," worthy of serious consideration.

26. Ibid.

27. **The International Protection of Minorities** (Minority Rights Group, Report No. 41, London, 1979), by James Fawcett, p. 4. This Report contains a Draft Convention on the Protection of Minorities, presented by the Minority Rights Group to the U.N. Human Rights Commission. More comprehensive than the Yugoslav draft, it would also grant group rights to minorities. The question of how the U.S.A. could contribute toward solving the international problem of minorities is ably discussed by Robert G. Wirsing's "The United States, and International Protetion of Minorities," Chapter 9 in Natalie Kaufman Hevener (ed.), **The Dynamics of Human Rights in U.S. Foreign Policy** (New Brunswick, N.J.: Transaction Books, 1981). See in particular pp. 186-193.

IV. Trianon and the Problem of National Minorities

The century preceding the outbreak of World War I was characterized by the spreading and intensification of nationalism on the one hand, and by the determined, sometimes ruthless, campaigns for the suppression of national movements on the other. Consequently, at the outbreak of the war the nationality question was one of the major unresolved problems in international relations and one of the most burning domestic issues in multi-national states. In order to satisfy nationalist aspirations at the war's end, the principle of national self-determination was brought to the fore. According to a perceptive observer, the Paris Peace Conference "allowed and sponsored the operation of that principle in a number of cases, chiefly where it worked to the disadvantage of the defeated powers, but admitted other factors as coordinate and, in some cases, overriding elements in the determination of frontiers. The principle of 'one nation, one state' was not realized to the full extent permitted by the ethnographic configuration of Europe, but it was approximated more closely than ever before."[1]

Unfortunately the half-hearted attempt to apply the principle of national self-determination did not eliminate the nationality problem. In fact, by permitting, or contributing to, the creation of new national minorities, it may have aggravated the problem. The case of Hungary serves as a good example.

The victorious Allied and Associated powers dismembered the Austro-Hungarian monarchy by creating a number of so-called "successor states." The idea was to replace the multi-national monarchy with smaller national states, who would jealously guard their newly-won independence and thereby prevent a possible future expansion of Germany into East Central Europe. History was to prove twenty years later that instead of ensuring peace for generations to come, the

52

peacemakers created a settlement that carried within itself the seeds of the Second World War and the Cold War. For the "successor states" were the least capable of checking Nazi aggression. Unwilling to satisfy the aspirations of their inordinately large national minorities, and concerned with preserving their territorial gains, they easily fell prey to Hitler's divide and conquer strategy, offering little significant resistance. Together with the greatly weakened and separated Austria and Hungary, the "successor states" became pawns on the chessboard of Nazi Germany and the Soviet Union.

Beyond doubt the Treaty of Trianon was the most severe of all post-war treaties. Its territorial impositions, disregarding the ethnic or linguistic borders, converted millions of Hungarians into minorities in supposed nation states. Before 1914 Hungary had a territory of 125,600 square miles. This is roughly half the size of Texas, or three times that of the state of Ohio. By the terms of the Treaty Hungary lost 89,700 square miles, or 71.4 percent of her former territory. Of her population of almost 21 million, 63.6 percent, including 3.3 million Hungarians, were detached. The inhabitants of dismembered Hungary numbered only 7.6 million on a territory of 35,900 square miles - the size of the state of Indiana. Romania alone received 39,800 square miles (almost the size of Ohio), more than what was left to Hungary. Czechoslovakia was presented with 23,800 square miles (equal to the size of West Virginia), and Yugoslavia received a similar slice, including Croatia - which for 800 years was associated with Hungary. Even Austria was allotted 1,500 square miles of Western Hungary, a slice of territory slightly larger than Rhode Island.2

By comparison, the Treaty of Versailles detached from Germany no more than 13 percent of its territory and 9.5 percent of its population. (The Peace of Frankfurt ending the Franco-Prussian War in 1871, had cost France a mere 2.6 percent of her territory and 4.1 percent of her population.) Having decreed that a multi-national state such as Austria-Hungary was not worthy of having a life of its own, the victors of World War I set up states such as Czechoslovakia, Yugoslavia, and Romania, which were multi-national states not unlike the old Empire.

Thus, the redrawing of the frontiers of the great polyglot empires of Eastern and Central Europe, and the limited reshuffling of populations, did by no means solve the problem of national minorities. The powers, in violation of proclaimed Wilsonian principles, handed over masses of people to alien sovereignties. Inis L. Claude, Jr. estimates the number to have been between 25 and 30 million, and a British authority on the question of national self-determination wrote as follows: "It was ironic that a settlement supposed to have been largely determined by the principle of nationality should have produced a state like Czechoslovakia, with minorities amounting to 34.7 percent of its population, quite apart from the question of the doubtful identity of nationality between Czechs and Slovaks. Poland was not much better off with minorities amounting to 30.4 percent ,or Romania, with 25 percent." 3

Altogether the "successor states" found themselves with 16 million persons belonging to national minorities, out of a total population of 42 million, while Hungary's new borders were far more restricted than the reach of her nationality. With her loss of territory, Hungary surrendered 1,663,576 Hungarians to Romania, 1,066,824 to Czechoslovakia, 571,735 to Yugoslavia, and 26,225 to Austria. Nearly two million of these lived just across the newly created borders, thus forming an integral part of the Hungarian ethnic bloc in the Danubian Basin, but now separated from it. According to Charles Seymour, the American delegate to the Peace Conference, the boundaries of the successor states in many cases did not even "roughly" correspond with ethnic or linguistic lines. In short, national self-determination was denied to the Hungarians.

A great deal was alleged about the treatment of the national minorities in Hungary. However, compared to the situation prevalent in the old Austro-Hungarian monarchy, the lot of the new national minorities was (and continues to be) miserable. "Is it not scandalous" - exclaimed Sir Robert Gower, Member of the House of Commons in Britain some 15 years after the peace settlement - "that a European reconstruction, loudly hailed as one that was going to liberate the national minorities, should have resulted in their persecution, the severity of which is such that there is no parallel to it to be found in the ancient Kingdom of Hungary, where the nationalities had been treated with infinitely more benevolence."4

Of the defeated, Hungary was punished the most

severely. Furthermore, none of the inhabitants of historic Hungary were given the right to decide their fate. When the Hungarian Peace Delegation was handed the terms of the treaty for signature, the chief of the delegation suggested that in accordance with the principle of self-determination the population affected by the treaty ought to be consulted through plebiscites. "Ask the peoples - on why the principle of self-determination was ignored at Trianon was that by the time the peacemakers turned to the treaty with Hungary they were bored with the entire process. In the words of one of the participants: "I am reliably informed that the delegates, and particularly the representatives of the Western Powers, are frightfully bored with the whole Peace Conference . . . Especially since we presented our notes and memoranda they have begun to realize that the Hungarian question should be examined from many angles for which they have neither time nor patience."

On the strength of the argument that Germany had been accorded the right of self-determination with regard to Schleswig-Holstein, Silesia, East Prussia, and the Saarland, the Chief Delegate of the Union of South Africa, General (later Prime Minister) Ian Smuts demanded that in connection with the proposed dismemberment of Hungary plebiscites be held in Transylvania, Slovakia, Ruthenia, and Croatia-Slavonia. At first a lone voice, he was later supported by the other British Dominions, as well as by Japan, Poland, and Italy. The fear of plebiscites, however, prevailed and they were denied. Some years later the Swiss historian and expert on minority affairs, Aldo Dami wrote: "A plebiscite refused is a plebiscite taken in fact."[6]

The Treaty of Trianon was signed on June 4, 1920. One year later, on June 7, 1921, the Reverend Father Weterle (for many years the protesting voice of Alsace in the German Imperial Parliament) declared in the French National Assembly: "I am profoundly convinced that had plebiscites been held, neither the Serbs nor the Rumanians would have received more than one-third of the votes cast. People have been pushed against their will. There can be no doubt about that."[7] Father Weterle spoke from experience; after all, the Alsatians, although of Germanic origin and language, desired to be French.

The Paris Peace Conference confused the concept of a

people's right to self-determination with the principle of defining nationality on the basis of language. The two are by no means identical; an ethnic group may well prefer to belong to a national sovereignty whose majority is linguistically different from its own. The Treaty of Trianon did in fact flout both principles by cutting off large blocs of purely Hungarian inhabited territories and awarding them to Hungary's neighbors for economic or strategic considerations. "The borders drawn at Trianon," asserts Aldo Dami, "excluded from Hungary a first zone of Hungarian territories, plus a second zone inhabited by non-Magyars whose interests were, however, so closely entwined with those of Hungary that there could have been no doubt of their decision, had they been consulted. Hence, the Peace of Trianon is based neither on ethnography nor on popular sentiment, nor even on the interests of the population concerned - which the latter are sure to know best."8

The concern with the protection of minorities originated in the religious sphere. Historically, international efforts to protect religious minorities against persecution took the form of ad hoc intervention by states on behalf of their co-religionists in other countries. Later practice included guarantees of freedom of religion for inhabitants of territories transferred to other countries by voluntary or forced cession. Occasionally, when religious division was identical with national division, such guarantee protected an entire nationality within a state.

The first express recognition and international guarantee of the rights of national minorities is found in the Final Act of the Congress of Vienna, in which Russia, Prussia, and Austria undertook to respect the nationality of their Polish subjects.9

The systematic protection of national minorities did not become a reality until the end of World War I and the establishment of the League of Nations. Even this system was limited in scope and applied only to special cases. A more comprehensive system, one with wider application, has not been established to this day.

As Clemenceau pointed out to Polish Prime Minister Ignacy Paderewski in his oft-quoted letter justifying the imposition of restrictions upon Poland's handling of national minorities, the Allied and Associated Powers felt a solemn obligation to protect those peoples whose future minority status was determined by decree. A plan for the international protection of national minorities appeared to be the only solution, and such a plan evolved out of a multiplicity of conflicting interests and points of view, and utilized an unprecedented set of international machinery: The League of Nations.10

The basis of the League of Nations system for the international protection of minorities consisted of a series of treaties, declarations, and conventions, whereby particular states accepted provisions relating to the treatment of minority groups and at the same time recognized the League as guarantor.

The international instruments, containing stipulations for the protection of minorities placed under the guarantee of the League of Nations, may be classified as follows:11

"Minorities" Treaties signed at Paris during the Peace Conference

Treaty between the Principal Allied and Associated Powers and Poland, signed at Versailles on June 28th, 1919.

Treaty between the Principal Allied and Associated Powers and the Kingdom of Serbs, Croats and Slovenes, signed at St. Germain on September 10th, 1919.

Treaty between the Principal Allied and Associated Powers and Czechoslovakia, signed at St. Germain on September 10th, 1919.

Treaty between the Principal Allied and Associated Powers and Romania, signed at Paris on December 9th, 1919.

Treaty between the Principal Allied and Associated Powers and Greece, signed at Sevres on August 10th, 1920.

Special Chapters inserted in the General Treaties of Peace

Treaty of Peace with Austria, signed at St. Germain-en-Laye on September 10th, 1919
(Part III, Section V, Articles 62 to 69).

Treat of Peace with Bulgaria; signed at Neuilly-sur-Seine on November 27th, 1919 (Part III, Section IV, Articles 49 to 57).

Treaty of Peace with Hungary, signed at Trianon on June 4th, 1920 (Part III, Section VI, Articles 54 to 60).

Treaty of Peace with Turkey, signed at Lausanne on July 24, 1923 (Part I, Section III, Articles 37 to 45).

Special Chapters inserted in other Treaties

German-Polish Convention on Upper Silesia, dated May 15th, 1922 (Part III).

Convention concerning the Memel Territory, dated May 8th, 1924 (Article II, and Articles 26 and 27 of the Statute annexed to the Convention).

Declarations made before the Council of the League of Nations

Declaration by Albania, dated October 2nd, 1921.
Declaration by Estonia, dated September 17th, 1923.
Declaration by Finland (in respect of the Aaland Islands), dated June 27th, 1921.
Declaration by Latvia, dated July 7th, 1923.
Declaration by Lithuania, dated May 12th, 1922.

Although different in form, all these instruments aimed at safeguarding the rights of "racial, religious or linguistic minorities." And the architects of the system made it clear that they regarded this designation as synonymous with "national minorities."[12]

The rights guaranteed to national minorities in the treaty-bound states fell into two categories: the rights of individuals as such, and the rights of individuals as members of a minority group. The safeguarding of the first category of rights demanded a system of negative equality -- protection against discrimination. The second category required, in addition, a regime of "positive equality" -- provisions for the equal opportunity of minorities to "preserve and develop their national culture and consciousness."[13] Nevertheless, these were still individual rights, arising out of membership in a minority and facilitating the maintenance and development of group life. Wilson and his fellow architects were too much imbued with the individualist traditions of liberalism to accept the concept of "group rights." The documents mentioned carefully avoided terminology from which it might have been inferred that minorities as corporate units were the "intended beneficiaries of the system."14 Claude notes only a few exceptions, such as Articles 9 and 10 of the Polish minority Treaty -- which could be interpreted as indirectly granting recognition to groups per se. Claude's cautious interpretation of the nature of minority rights is not shared by all. On the contrary, some say that the rights protected by the League were, at least in part, rights accorded to minorities as groups. Thus, André Mandelstam in his La Protection des Minorités distinguished between rights of minorities on an individual basis -- religious liberty, freedom of using their own language, freedom of education in their own language, freedom of association -- and rights of minorities as collective entities -- proportional representation in elective bodies, and autonomy.15

The League guarantee was collective; the task of enforcing the obligations of the concerned states was assigned to the organization, more specifically to the Council. In addition, although judicial procedures were available through the Permanent Court of International Justice, the guarantee, as established, was basically political in nature. It was part of the larger system designed to facilitate the maintenance of international peace.

In order to discharge its functions as a guarantor, the Council of the League developed certain operating procedures empirically (one might say "on a trial and error" method), starting with the suggestions contained in the Tittoni Report of 1920, and concluding with the 1929 report and the recommendations of a special committee headed by Adatci, the Japanese representative, who served as the Council's Rapporteur on minority questions. 16

In its final form the procedure consisted of five successive steps, namely:

Acceptance of Petitions (from minorities);
Communications to the Government concerned for any Observations;
Communication to the Members of the Council;
Examination by the Committee of Three (Council Members); and
Replies to Petitioners

Given the stringent qualifications that had to be met for each successive step, and the half-hearted support the system enjoyed in the Council, this so-called "petition system" functioned with only limited success. Its failures and deficiencies were numerous. According to one of its many critics: "It is impossible to maintain that the minorities obtained an adequate and impartial hearing of their grievances and demands, or prompt, effective, and reliable measures of protection . . . The League system was superior to possible alternative arrangements relying exclusively upon internal constitutional guarantees of minority rights, or resting upon bilateral agreements unsupported by an international guarantee, or leaving the protection of minorities dependent upon the unregulated and capricious intervention of kin-states; but it was unable to solve the difficult problem with which it came to grips."17

Basically, the League system was unpopular with all those concerned for a variety of reasons. The states with minorities disliked it because it limited their "sovereign rights." The minorities disliked it, because it was cumbersome and did not provide the protection desired. The kin-states were dissatisfied with the system because they were excluded from it altogether. Moreover, it was a system affecting a few states only, rather than a general one affecting all. This proved to be very irksome to those who were placed under its obligations, while other nations, though they possessed minorities, were totally excluded. Czechoslovakia for one was willing to cooperate, Poland was resentful, and produced in 1934 a statement that amounted to a virtual denunciation of minority obligations. On September 13, 1934, Colonel Beck announced to the Assembly of the League that "pending the introduction of a general and uniform system for the protection of minorities, his Government was compelled to refuse, as from that day, all co-operation with the international organizations in the matter of the supervision of the application by Poland of the system of minority protection."18

Following this declaration, the League system of minority protection became increasingly ineffectual, until it was ultimately swept away by the events of World War II.

*   *   *

The problems of national minorities, which the peacemakers left unresolved, continue even today, sixty years after the Treaty of Trianon came into force. Attempts to reduce the scope of the minorities problem by revising the borders drawn in the Treaty have been in vain. The only frontier revisions were those performed by the Axis Powers immediately prior to and during World War II. In the case of Hungary the two Vienna Awards resulted in a new border that followed more closely than before the ethnic or linguistic line. However, these border revisions were declared null and void by the Paris Peace Treaties of 1947. Unlike the treaties of 1919 and 1920, those of 1947 did not even provide for the protection of national minorities.

As a result, hundreds of thousands of Hungarians have been expelled from lands where they were born and where they lived, and millions of others remain oppressed minorities. Their case has been presented repeatedly to the United Nations and other international forums. The U.S. Congress held numerous hearings on the subject. Documents, letters, memoranda smuggled out from Czechoslovakia, Romania, Yugoslavia, and the Soviet Union, tell of wholesale violation of human rights of the national minorities.

Deeply moved by the plight of the oppressed East-Central European national minorities, and in possession of overwhelming documentation to plead their case, spokesmen for the American Hungarian community, in observing the sixtieth anniversary of the Treaty of Trianon, called on the President and Congress of the United States to do all that is possible for the protection of human rights and the rights of national or ethnic minorities in Czechoslovakia, Romania, Yugoslavia, as well as the Soviet Union. "Let the United States continue to be the champion of freedom and human dignity in the world, so as to maintain in high esteem the country and the ideals admired by the oppressed everywhere."[19]

One glimmer of hope for the protection of national minorities on a world-wide basis appeared on the horizon in May, 1978, when the United Nations Commission on Human Rights in Geneva transmitted a number of documents dealing with minority rights to the governments of the member nations. One of the documents was a "Draft Declaration on the Rights of Persons Belonging to National, Ethnic, Religious and Linguistic

Minorities" submitted by the government of Yugoslavia for discussion.20

It will be years before we know whether the proposal for a declaration on minority rights has sufficient world-wide support to survive the cumbersome and politically motivated procedures of the United Nations system. If it does, it will be only a first step toward creating a more binding international convention. Nevertheless, after a rather long period of neglect, the sentiments of the international community at present appear to be on the side of minorities.

NOTES:

1. Inis L. Claude, Jr., **National Minorities: An International Problem** (Cambridge: Harvard University Press, 1955), p. 12.

2. For additional comparative data see Yves de Daruvar, **The Tragic Fate of Hungary** (Munich: Nemzetor, 1974), pp. 99-106.

3. Alfred Cobban, **The Nation State and National Self-Determination** (London: Collins, 1969). p. 86

4. Sir Robert Gower, **La Revision du Traite de Trianon** (Paris, 1937), p. 16, quoted by Daruvar, p. 111.

5. Quoted by Daruvar, p. 92.

6. Ibid.

7. Daruvar, p. 93.

8. Aldo Dami, **La Hongrie de Demain** (Paris, 1932), p. 133, quoted by Daruvar, p. 93.

9. For the wording of this undertaking in the original French see C.A. Macartney, **National States and National Minorities**, 2nd ed. (New York: Russell, 1968), p. 160.

10. The text of Clemenceau's letter is reproduced in Oscar 1. Janowsky, **Nationalities and National Minorities** (New York: Macmillan, 1945), p. 179-84.

11. Pablo de Azcarate y Florez, **League of Nations and National Minorities** (New York: Carnegie Endowment, 1945) appendix. A complete collection of these instruments is found in League of Nations, **Protection of Linguistic, Racial and Religious Minorities by the League of Nations**, 1927. I.B.2.

12. Claude, p. 17, referring to The Public Papers of Woodrow Wilson, I. 463, 543.

13. Pablo de Azcarate y Florez, p. 82.

14. Claude, p. 19.

15. Andre Mandelstam, **La Protection des Minorites** (Paris: Hachette,

1925), p. 53-70.

16. Adatci's Report is reproduced in full in the Appendix to Pablo de Azcarate y Florez, **League of Nations and National Minorities** (New York: Carnegie Endowment, 1945). Azcarate was head of the League's Minority Section.

17. Claude, p. 30; and see his Chapter 3, "The Failure of the League Minority System." Detailed criticism is also offered by Macartney, chapter 10, and by F.P. Walters, **A History of the League of Nations** (London: Oxford University Press, 1965), Chapter 34. The operating procedure is described in detail in the Adatci Report. A good legal analysis of the Minority Treaty obligations is to be found in Andre Mandelstam, **La Protection des Minorites.**

18. Macartney, p. 503.

19. **U. S. Congressional Record**, Vol. 126, No. 118 (July 28, 1980), p. E. 3633.

20. United Nation Document E/CN.4/L.1367/Rev. 1. The Draft Declaration was discussed at the 34th Session of the Commission on Human Rights in the spring of 1978. Eventually, after each government reacts in writing, it will reach the General Assembly.

V. THE ETHNIC PRINCIPLE AND NATIONAL BOUNDARIES

A CASE STUDY OF THE CZECHOSLOVAK-HUNGARIAN BORDER DISPUTE OF 1938

The roots of the Czechoslovak-Hungarian border dispute of 1938 reach back to the Paris Peace Settlements following World War I. The Treaty of Trianon reduced Hungary proper to less than one third of her former territory and about two-fifths of her population. Large numbers of Magyars were attached to the newly created "Successor States", without consulting the population of the territories transferred. Hungary maintained from the beginning the position that she would seek to change the terms of the Treaty by all available peaceful means as it was not a negotiated, but an "imposed" treaty, and as such, it was unjust. Her main hope was the League of Nations, a new organization which was thought to be capable of correcting all the mistakes committed by the peacemakers. Instead, the League became an instrument of the victorious powers to preserve the status quo . Consequently, Hungary began to orient her foreign policy toward the anti-status quo Powers; first toward Italy, who was openly sponsoring the Hungarian revisionist case, and after the annexation of Austria, toward her new neighbor, Germany. In 1938 Hungary definitely abandoned the idea of seeking peaceful revision through the procedure envisaged by Article XIX of the Covenant. Instead, she joined the policies of Germany and Poland. The aim of the three states was similar: the attainment of a favorable settlement of their minorities' question with Czechoslovakia.

The opening was provided by the Munich Agreement, signed by the Big Four on September 29, 1938, as a result of

64

the changing European distribution of power. The agreement arranged for the cession of the Sudeten areas of Czechoslovakia to Germany. It also called for the settlement of the Polish and Hungarian minority questions through direct negotiations. While Poland achieved her aims within days by presenting an ultimatum to Prague, Hungary entered into direct negotiations. These, however, failed for reasons to be explained below. Ultimately, at the wish of the two parties the matter was referred to Italo-German arbitration. Foreign Ministers Galeazzo Ciano and Joachim von Ribbentrop arbitrated the dispute, the latter supporting the Slovak, the former the Hungarian case. The arbitral award was based almost exclusively on ethnographic factors and restored to Hungary 12,103 square kilometers (approximately 4,630 square miles) of territory with slightly over one million population, eighty percent Magyars.

These are in brief the facts of the case. Looking back in a perspective of thirty-five years the question arises: was the application of the ethnic principle to the delimitation of the new border a wise choice? Was it politically sound?

The answer will be sought in three steps:

First, by looking at the actual negotiations between the parties.
Second, by looking at the arbitration.
Third, by evaluating the arbitral award and its consequences.

1.THE NEGOTIATIONS: CLAIMS AND COUNTERCLAIMS

The delegates of the disputants convened at Komárom (Komárno) on October 9, 1938. Hungary was represented by Foreign Minister Kalman Kánya and by Count Paul Teleki, Minister of Education, a well known cartographer and scholar of ethnic problems. The two were assisted by a staff of experts, armed with statistics and maps. The Czechoslovak delegation consisted entirely of Slovaks. The latter, having declared the autonomy of Slovakia three days before, insisted that the Slovak frontiers were their concern. The delegation was lead by Msgr.

Tiso, Prime Minister of Slovakia, and included Minister Jan Durcansky and Dr. Ivan Krno, Political Director of the Czechoslovak Ministry of Foreign Affairs. In the absence of delegates from Ruthenia, the latter was represented by Ivan Parkanyi, Ruthenian Minister in the Prague Cabinet.

The Hungarians decided to ask for the same terms that were given to Germany in Munich: ethnic frontiers on the basis of the census of 1910, and plebiscites in the contested areas. They asked for the unconditional cession of the ethnically Magyar areas and they put forward a demand for plebiscites in the remainder of Slovakia and Ruthenia hoping that, if accepted, the Slovaks might, and the Ruthenes certainly would, vote for a return to Hungary. The Slovaks, in turn, insisted that the question of the future of Slovakia and Ruthenia fell outside the scope of the Munich Agreement. They were unwilling to discuss this matter.

There remained the ethnic claims of Hungary. The Slovaks did not argue the principle but were unable to agree on the figures presented by their opponents. In the course of the protracted discussions the Hungarians presented the following case:

The Treaty of Trianon had granted to Czechoslovakia 62,937 square kilometers, or 22 per cent of Hungary's territory and according to the census of 1910, 3,575,685 persons of whom 1,702,000, or 46.6 per cent, were Slovaks; 1,084,000, or 30 per cent, Hungarians; 436,000, or 12 per cent, Ruthenes; 266,000, or 7.5 per cent, Germans; 22,000 Romanians, and 68,000 others.1

According to Hungarian statistics, the territory transferred to Czechoslovakia counted 13 towns and 830 villages where the Hungarians surpassed the 50 per cent proportion. The total territory of these towns and villages was 12,316 square kilometers. In 1910 they had a total population of 907,278, of whom 818,401, or 90.2 per cent were of Hungarian nationality; 51,373, or 5.7 per cent were of Slovak nationality, and 19,641, or 2.2 per cent were Germans.

The Hungarians transmitted to the Slovak delegation the map of the Magyar ethnic zone alongside the border, with the requested new frontier marked. The line proposed by Hungary included twelve out of the thirteen towns and 812 out of the 830 villages with Hungarian majority. Counterbalancing the villages of Hungarian majority that fell beyond the requested line, there were several villages of Slovak or mixed population on the Hungarian side, for one reason, "because of their enclaved situation, for another, to trace the new borderline as reasonably as possible."2

The territory of which the retrocession was asked measured 14,153 square kilometers with a population counting 1,090,569 inhabitants of whom 848,969, or 77.9 per cent, were of Hungarian nationality, 147,294, or 13.5 per cent were of Slovak nationality, and 63,927, or 5.9 per cent were Germans.

Beyond doubt, there existed an ethnic line, by and large coinciding with the geographical line where the foothills of the mountains ended and the plain began. In the rural areas north of this line the population was Slovak, to the south, Hungarian. Nevertheless, in the towns that lay in the mouths of the valleys exactly on the ethnic line, the population was very mixed and included people who were bilingual or of mixed origin. These could equally well be described as belonging to either nationality.

In addition, there were a large number of Jews whom both regimes counted on their own side for statistical purposes. Thus, with regard to the string of towns of which Hungary had asked the restitution, the ethnic line was blurred. Accordingly, the towns were hotly contested.3

The first proposition of the Slovak delegation consisted only of a promise of autonomy of the Hungarians of Slovakia within the Czechoslovak State. As Prague had already accepted the principle of cession of the ethnic areas, this offer seems to have originated exclusively with the Slovak Autonomous Government. The delegation pointed out in support of this offer that the Munich Agreement did not exclude such a solution. The offer was rejected at once by Kánya, who said that "he had come to negotiate, not to joke."4

After the Hungarian refusal to accept autonomy the Slovak delegation demanded a short interruption; subsequently it offered the "Velky Ostrov Zitny", or "Csallokoz", the island surrounded by the branches of the Danube between Bratislava and Komárom. The area of the island of Csallokoz was 1,840 square kilometers with a population of 121,000, of whom

117,000 were Hungarians. This offer, too was rejected by Hungary.

As the next step the Slovak delegation made a new offer on October 13, carrying, according to Hungarian figures, a total area of 5,405 square kilometers where the population in 1910 numbered 349,026 inhabitants, 341,987 of them Hungarians.

According to the terms of this offer 724,698 persons of Hungarian nationality would have remained in Czechoslovak territory. The second Slovak territorial offer represented only 38.3 per cent of the territory and 31.7 per cent of the population demanded by Hungary.

On their side and on the base of the statistics of 1930, the Slovaks maintained that according to the Hungarian demands, Slovakia would have to cede 11,268 square kilometers of her territory with 1, 120,000 inhabitants, and Carpatho-Ruthenia 1,982 square kilometers with a population of 218,000 inhabitants. Thus, by surrendering to Hungary 670,000 Hungarians, Slovakia and Ruthenia would lose more than 650,000 inhabitants of Slavic race.

The second Slovak territorial offer was geared to the above estimates. According to the Slovak delegation the second territorial offer proposed to cede to Hungary 5,784 square kilometers with 395,000 inhabitants, among them 45,000 Slovaks. The 300,000 Hungarians still to remain in Slovakia would have balanced the Slovak minority living in Hungary, estimated by the Slovak delegation to be 300,000.

The deadlock . During the negotiations, the Hungarians had repeatedly pointed out that, contrary to the assertions of the Slovaks, ethnic conditions outside the actual border zone were irrelevant. In the Hungarian view, the Slovaks south of the main ethnic line, including a considerable number in central Hungary, were descendants of voluntary immigrants. They were citizens of Hungary who did not desire to join Czechoslovakia, and their Magyarization was spontaneous. At any rate, the Hungarian figure of those who declared themselves to be Slovaks according to mother tongue was only 104,819 in 1930.[5]

In addition, Teleki argued that the Czechoslovak proposals were based on economic, not ethnic considerations.[6] According to him the past twenty years proved that only the frontiers based on ethnic considerations are stable ones. Ways and means could always be found, Teleki said, to solve the problems of trade and traffic, if there was good will.

Although they rejected the proposals as insufficient, both Kánya and Teleki were inclined to continue the negotiations. They believed that the Slovaks would offer still another proposal.7 But the Hungarian Prime Minister Imrédy, impatient and nervous, declared that the gulf was "too wide to be bridged", and ordered his delegation to break off the negotiations abruptly.8

2. The Arbitration of the Dispute

Following the breakdown of direct negotiations, Foreign Minister Ribbentrop held conversations with both sides, and persuaded them to resume negotiations through regular diplomatic channels. Interestingly, the Slovaks did not reject the 1910 census as a basis of settlement; they merely complained that the data presented by the Hungarians was "incorrect." They also asked Ribbentrop to support their proposals "especially for reasons of communication and economics."9 The Hungarians were willing to consider a new proposal, and suggested that if the latter were still unacceptable, the dispute be submitted to Italo-German mediation or arbitration.10

On October 22, 1938, Prague forwarded a new proposal to Budapest. This third territorial offer envisaged the cession of a territory of 11,300 square kilometers, registering, according to the 1910 census, 740,000 inhabitants; according to the 1930 census, 850,000 inhabitants. The new proposals came rather close to the original demand of the Hungarians.

Budapest expressed its satisfaction, but countered the note on October 24 with some amendments. According to these amendments the area now offered by Czechoslovakia was to be considered as undisputed, as well as to be occupied by Hungary immediately. The area still in dispute north of the suggested line, and engulfing the important towns, was to be divided into eight zones as plebiscite areas under international supervision. Pressburg was to be set aside for special conversations, and the Ruthenes were to decide on their own future.11

On Oct. 26, Prague informed London that the Hungarian demand for plebiscites in the disputed areas on the basis of the 1910 census was unacceptable. Prague favored Axis arbitration and "wished to have the views of His Majesty's Government on their attitude."12 In reply, the Czechoslovak Government was informed that "His Majesty's Government saw no objection to the Czech-Hungarian question by means of arbitration by Germany and Italy, if the Czechoslovak and Hungarian Governments agreed to settle their differences this way." It was added that, "if the two parties to the dispute preferred to refer the matter to the four Munich Powers, His Majesty's Government would be ready to join in any discussion."13 Similar information was forwarded to the British Embassy at Rome for the benefit of Signor Mussolini.14

Prague was now ready to answer the Hungarian counter-proposals. The Czechoslovak note of October 26 passed entirely in silence over the proposed Hungarian occupation of the "undisputed" territories. There was no reference to the proposed plebiscites. The note emphatically asserted that the problem related to the Hungarian minority only and added that, since the Hungarian Government did not accept the Czechoslovak proposals as they were, "the Czechoslovak Government agreed to submit the question of the Hungarian minority to an arbitral decision by Germany and Italy, signatories of the Munich Agreement."15 Finally, the note stated that in case the two Powers accepted Hungary's proposal to include Poland, Czechoslovakia wished to include Rumania as an arbiter.

Surprised about the proposal to submit the entire question to arbitration, the Hungarian Government replied on October 27. The reply attempted once more to extend the application of the right of self-determination by way of a plebiscite to all minorities requesting it. On the question of German-Italian arbitration the note stressed that its acceptance "implies the obligation to submit in advance to the decision of the said Powers." The note then continued:

"It is understood that the competence of the arbiters extends only to the   territories in dispute and not to those on which agreement already exists between the two Governments and the occupation of which by the Hungarian troops was alrcady askcd in thc note of 24th current."16

Foreign Minister Chvalkovsky answered on October 28 in a polite note. The question was that of the Hungarian minority only. He noted with satisfaction that Hungary agreed to resort to arbitration by Germany and Italy with the obligation to submit in advance to the decision. Czechoslovakia placed full confidence in this procedure which had been suggested, according to Chvalkovsky, by the Hungarian Government itself.17

Chvalkovsky could not share the view of the Hungarian Government that an agreement existed already on certain territories and proposed that the arbitrators pronounce also on this difference of views. He was sure that the question of occupation, referred to the Hungarian note of October 27, would be regulated by the arbitral decision.

Finally, as a practical step Chvalkovsky suggested that the two Governments make a request within twenty-four hours to Germany and Italy to undertake the arbitration. Thereupon Hungary, until now only saying that she was prepared to do so, lodged her formal request in Berlin and in Rome for arbitration. Czechoslovakia did the same.

Decision in the Belvedere. The arbitral session opened in the Belvedere Palace in Vienna, on November 2, 1938, at noon. After the opening remarks by Ribbentrop and Ciano, the Hungarians and Czechs pleaded their cause. Kanya was "bitter and argumentative", Teleki was "calm and with more documentation." Chvalkovsky was brief and left the task of presenting the Czechoslovak case to Minister Krno. In the view of Ciano, the Czechoslovaks "defended their cause well."18

The arguments presented in the course of the pleadings were not different from the ones already propounded during the previous negotiations. Lacking German support, Hungary did not raise the question of Pressburg, nor that of the two easternmost towns, Ungvar and Munkacs, all of which had a mixed population. The question of Nitra and Kassa was debated at some length. The discussions seemed to prove in general the difficulty of settlement along ethnic lines, especially where historical considerations were also at play.19

The two arbiters continued their conversations with the delegates during lunch, then retired with a small staff to prepare the Award. Ciano took control of the discussions and, except for a few disputed points, was able to trace the new frontier. Ribbentrop's unpreparedness enabled Ciano "to assign to Hungary pieces of territory which might easily have given rise to much controversial discussion."[20]

The day was closed by the reading and afterwards the signing of the arbitral award and the accompanying protocol. By virtue of the terms thus rendered, Czechoslovakia retained in the western section of Slovakia the towns of Bratislava and Nitra. Hungary recovered the three disputed eastern towns in addition to four others in the central section.[21]

The area awarded to Hungary comprised 12,103 square kilometers (approximately 4,600 square miles) with a population of 1,030,000 inhabitants. The population breakdown differs according to the relevant censuses. To compensate for this difference, the British Ambassador to Hungary, Sir G. Knox, who thought that both censuses had a political basis, gave the Foreign Office figures which were believed to be approximately accurate.

The figures of Knox were:[22]

Hungarians	830,000
Slovaks	140,000
Germans	20,000
Others*	50,000
Total:	1,030,000

*Ruthenes, Poles, Rumanians

Thus, the number of Hungarians in Czechoslovakia diminished to 66,000. At the same time, the ration of Hungary's non-Magyar population had increased from 7.2 per cent to approximately 9 per cent.

Conforming to plans worked out by a Czechoslovak-Hungarian commission of military experts, the ceded area was occupied by Hungary between the 5th and 10th of November as stipulated by the Award. On the latter date, the line of demarcation was fixed by the military commission.

EVALUATION OF THE AWARD
AND ITS CONSEQUENCES

Throughout the entire dispute there was a conspicuous absence of legal claims and considerations. The dispute was markedly political in its character. Generally speaking, whenever the arguments of the parties are intended to demonstrate, respectively, that they have title to a territory, the dispute is classified as "legal."23 In contrast to the former there are disputes where, instead of trying to prove that they do own, the parties argue that they should be allowed to own the disputed territory. They appeal to considerations outside and above the law. Their claims are economic, strategic, ethnic or historical claims, so-called "non-legal claims to territory."

In the case of the Czechoslovak-Hungarian controversy the issues of the dispute and the scope of the arbitration were, as we had seen, defined through political processes.

Hungary insisted at first not only to ethnographic revision, but also on self-determination for Slovakia and Ruthenia. She derived considerable support from Poland. The main purpose of Hungary in pursuing this course seems to have been the desire to displace the French-sponsored Little Entente by the weakening of Czechoslovakia.

Poland thought that the annexation of Ruthenia by Hungary would create a common barrier against Germany, remove an important centre for Ukrainian nationalism, and permit the formation of a front against communism.24

The weakening of the Little Entente was likewise a purpose of both Germany and Italy. Germany's chief concern was, of course, Czechoslovakia. Willing to see an ethnic revision there, Germany had denied Hungary's larger claims for political and military reasons. Hitler told the Slovak Ministers on March 13, 1939:

"I approved of the Vienna Award in the conviction that the Slovaks would   separate themselves from the Czechs and declare their independence, which would be under German protection. That is why I refused the Hungarian demands in respect of Slovakia."25

Italy on her part pursued a policy of alienating Yugoslavia from the Little Entente, and increasing her own

73

influence in Yugoslavia, as well as in Rumania. This policy had a strong anti-French overtone.

Britain and France, once they consented to the inclusion of the Sudeten Germans into Germany, could not refuse ethnic revision in favor of Hungary. Finally, the revision on ethnic lines in Czechoslovakia was acceptable to Yugoslavia and Rumania for two reasons. First, neither of them possessed a territory that contained overwhelmingly Magyar population and at the same time was contiguous with Hungary. Second, with the balance of power having turned in favor of the Axis, both States were eager to show a cooperating attitude. Thus, while a revision on ethnic lines was thought to result in a more equitable frontier for Hungary, the selection of the ethnic principle was based primarily on political considerations. Political considerations played a part in the selection of arbitrators as well. The confidence of the Slovak leaders in a decision by Germany in their favor was instrumental in bringing about German-Italian arbitration.26

As soon as the larger claims of Hungary had been eliminated and the ethnic principle was accepted, Hungary adjusted herself to the new situation, the reason being that a revision of this type was still in conformity with the interests and aims of Hungarian policy. By drawing the frontier on strictly ethnic lines the Hungarian Government hoped to create a situation whereby geographic and economic considerations would, in due course, induce the Ruthenes, and perhaps the Slovaks, to seek re-entry into Hungary.27

Once the desirability of the ethnic frontier was established, the main effort of the Hungarian Government was concentrated on excluding all economic considerations from the settlement. This course of action enjoyed the full support of the Italian and, in the final stage, of the German Governments. The strict application of the ethnic principle in the Vienna Award was in conspicuous contrast to the application of the principle of self-determination at the Paris Peace Conference of 1919. On the latter occasion, the principle was, in the delineation of Czechoslovak-Hungarian frontiers, at times severely ignored in favor of economic and strategic considerations, and in general to the disadvantage of Hungary.

The drawing of the frontier well to the south of the ethnic

line in Western Slovakia was explained by the necessity of granting Czechoslovakia access to the sea by extending her territory to the Danube River. The line in the central sector was dictated, according to Dr. Benes, by railway communications.28

The latter consideration, supported by the French and the British, took priority over the vital consideration of including the smallest possible number of Magyars within Czechoslovakia, a view advanced by the American and Italian delegates.29

Finally, Ruthenia, which was to become an autonomous State within "Czecho-Slovakia", was included in order to provide a common frontier and railway communications with Rumania.30 In the end the boundaries of Czechoslovakia, to use the expression of Charles Seymour, American delegate to the conference, did not even "roughly" correspond with the ethnic or linguistic line.31

The settlement of 1938 displayed the opposite characteristics. In this regard, the British historian R. W. Seton-Watson noted the following:

"For the restoration of the Danube island and the district around Nove Zamky and Levice, where the population is overwhelmingly Magyar, a good case could be made out, though it meant cutting off Slovakia from access to the Danube, save for a few kilometers to the east of Bratislava. On a purely ethnographic basis the Magyars were entitled to recover the towns of Rimavska Sobota and Roznava, though the result has been to render communications by road and rail impossible along the whole southern border of Slovakia. But by the cession of Kosice Slovakia had been deprived of its second capital, the natural and only possible economic and cultural centre of the whole eastern half of Slovak territory; and this was done on the basis of the census of 1910".32

The province Ruthenia was deprived of its two principal towns, Ungvar (Uzhorod) and Munkacs (Mukacevo), and of the whole of its fertile territory, to the west of those two towns without which she was practically unable to exist. Ruthenia retained in fact, only the mountainous region in the north, while its system of communications with Slovakia had been completely dislocated.33 Without doubt, the ethnic principle had been applied "generously in Hungary's favor."34 The noted expert on East-Cetnral Europe, Hugh Seton-Watson remarked that "the frontier between Hungary and Slovakia could be drawn on lines more generous to Hungary than 1920 while less unfair to the Slovaks than 1938".[35]

The strict application of the ethnic principle in the Vienna Award produced therefore, a frontier, which although more equitable from the ethnic view than that drawn in 1919, was largely unreasonable. According to some critics the principle of national self-determination was again used as a principle of disintegration[36] . In this sense, then, the 1938 settlement presents only a slight improvement over previous cases, and we are still faced with the question: Can the ethnic principle be applied in a manner whereby it unites, rather than divides, different peoples?

NOTES:

1. These and the following data are from the documentary collection Andre Balasko (ed.), "Frontieres Tchecoslovaques", **La Documentation Internationale Politique, Juridique et Economique**, Vl (Mars-Avril 1939), pp. 26-28. Hereafter cited as La Documentation.

2. Ibid., p.26.

3. Carlyle A. Macartney, **A History of Hungary 1929-1945**, Vol 1. (New York: Frederick A. Praeger, 1957), p. 285. Proceeding from West to East the Contested towns and cities were Pozsony (Bratislava), Nyitra (Nitra), Leva (Levice), Losonc (Lucenec), Rimaszombat (Rimavska Sobota), Rozsnyo (Roznava), Kassa (Kosice), Ungvar (Uzhorod), Munkacs (Mukacevo), and Huszt (Chust). Macartney gives a brief, but valuable, summary of the entire dispute.

4. Royal Institute of InternationalAffairs, **Survey of International Affairs 1938**, Vol. III. (London: Oxford University Press,1951) . p.85. This particular volume of the **Survey** contains a detailed description and analysis of the dispute and its solution.

5. Stephen D. Kertesz, Diplomacy in a Whirlpool; **Hungary between Nazi Germany and Soviet Russia** (South Bend: University of Notre Dame Press,1953), p.270.

6. The Czechoslovaks afterwards told Newton, British Ambassador, that the proposals had been based "on ethnical results of the 1930 census tempered where necessary by strategic, economic and transit considerations" to be worked out on a reciprocal basis. E.L. Woodward and Rohan Butler (eds.), **Documents on British Foreign Policy 1919-1939**, 3rd Series, Vol. III (London: His Majesty's Stationery Office,1950), p.171. Hereafter cited as **British Documents**.

7. This assumption later proved to be right. Newton was told by the Czechs that the second territorial offer "had not been submitted as their last word." **Ibid.**

8. Had he waited just a little longer, he might have come to an advantageous arrangement with the Ruthenes, for during the days of the conference events in Ruthenia took a turn quite favorable for Hungary. The two political groupings, namely the more or less pro-Hungarian Ruthene Council and the Slavophile Ukrainian Council finally reached an agreement about the future of Ruthenia, proposing to demand a plebiscite for the whole area, rather than to have it partitioned. The head of the newly formed coalition government, the strongly pro-Hungarian Mr. Brody, insisted on his right to represent Ruthenia at the negotiations. Prepared to make a deal with the Hungarians independently of the Slovaks, Brody flew to Komarom on October 13. He arrived just in time to see the two delegations part in anger. Macartney, p. 287.

9. U.S. Department of State, **Documents on Germany Foreign Policy 1918-1945.** From the Archives of the German Foreign Ministry. Series D (1937-45), Vol. IV (Washington: U.S. Government Printing Office,1949-1956), p.87. Hereafter cited as **German Documents.**

10. Ibid. p.80.

11. **La Documentation**, p.29.

12. **British Documents**, III, 202.

13. **Ibid.**

14. **Ibid.**, p. 203.

15. **La Documentation**, p.30.

16. **Ibid.**, pp.30-31.

17. **La Documentation**, pp.30-31.

18. Galeazzo, Ciano, **Hidden Diary 1937-1938,** trans. Andreas Mayor (New York: F.P. Dutton and Co., 1953), entry for November 3, 1938.

19. For a detailed description of the pleadings see "Documents on the Vienna Award", **German Documents**, IV, 118-124.

20. Ciano, **Diary**, Nov.3. Cf. Erich Kordt, **Nicht aus den Akten...**, (Stuttgart, Union Deutsche Verlagsgesellschafft: 1950), p. 287.

21. See map.

22. **British Documents**, III, 181.

23. In international practice the following titles are recognized by States: occupation, accretion, prescription, cession, and conquest. They are called "legal claims" to territory. Cf. Charles Fenwick, **International Law**, (3rd ed; New York: Appleton,1954), p.343.

24. **British Documents**, III, 238.

25. International Military Tribunal, **Trial of the Major War Criminals Before the International Military Tribunal**, Vol. XXXV (Nuremberg: I.M.T., 1949), p.175.

26. This was confirmed later. Cf. Jozef Lettrich, **History of Modern Slovakia** (New York: Praeger, 1955), p. 103.

27. **Survey**, III,70.

28. Francis Deak, **Hungary at the Paris Peace Conference** (New York: Columbia University Press, 1942), pp. 28, 35, 36.

29. **Deak**, p. 45

30. **Ibid.**, pp. 35, ff.

31. E.M. House and C. Seymour, **What Really Happened at Paris?** (New York: Charles Scribner's Sons, 1921), p. 103.

32. R. W. Seton-Watson, **From Munich to Danzig.** (London: Methuen & co.,1939), pp.116-117.

33. Hubert Ripka, Munich: **Before and After.** A **Fully Documented Czechoslovak Account of the Crises of September 1938 and March 1939** (London: Victor Gollancz Ltd.,1939) pp. 202, 204.

34. Elizabeth Wiskemann, **Prologue to War** (London: Oxford University Press, 1945). p. 21.

35. Hugh Seton-Watson, **Eastern Europe Between the Wars, 1918-1941** (Cambridge: The University Press, 1945), p. 349

36. Alfred Cobban, **National Self-Determination** (Chicago: University of Chicago Press, 1947). p. 42.

APPENDIX

DOCUMENTS

COMISSION ON HUMAN RIGHTS,
THIRTHY-FOURTH SESSION

DRAFT DECLARATION BY YUGOSLAVIA

Rights of Persons Belonging to National,
Ethnic, Religious and Linguistic Minorities

The General Assembly,

Recognizing that one of the basic aims of the United Nations is to promote and enhance the respect for human rights and the fundamental freedoms for all, without distinction as to race, sex, language or religion,

Bearing in mind international instruments relating to human rights, including the rights of national, ethnic, linguistic or religious minorities, such as the International Covenant on Civil and Political Rights, the International Convention on the Elimination of All Forms of Racial Discrimination, the Convention of the United Nations Educational, Scientific and Cultural Organization against Discrimination in Education, the Convention of the International Labour Organization concerning Discrimination in Respect of Employment and Occupation, as well as the instruments adopted at the regional level and concluded between individual States Members of the United Nations,

Considering that the friendly relations and co-operation among States in the spirit of the Declaration on Principles of International Law concerning Friendly Relations and Co-operation among States in accordance with the Charter of the United Nations, contribute to international peace and stabiliy and to the creation of more favourable conditions for the realization and promotion of the right of national, ethnic, linguistic or religious minorities, and that the realization and promotion of the rights of minorities, in turn, contributes to friendship and co-operation among peoples and States,

Recognizing the need to ensure even more effective implementation of the existing instruments of international law relating to the rights of national, ethnic, linguistic or religious minorities,

Bearing in mind the work done so far within the United Nations system, in particular by the Commission on Human Rights and the Sub-Commission on the Prevention of Discrmination and Protection of

80

Minorities, on securing and promoting the rights of minorities, and the need for further efforts aimed at ensuring and promoting the rights of national, ethnic, linguistic or religious minorities,

Proclaims this Declaration on the Rights of National, Ethnic, Linguistic or Religious Minorities:

Article 1

National, ethnic, linguistic or religious minorities (hereinafter: minorities) have the right to existence, to the respect for, and the promotion of, their own national, cultural, linguistic and other characteristics and to enjoyment of full equality in relation to the rest of the population, regardless of their number.

Article 2

1. Members of minorities shall enjoy all human rights and the fundamental freedoms without any discrimination as to national, ethnic or racial origin, language or religion .

2. Any propaganda or activity aimed at discriminating against minorities or threatening their right to equal expression and development of their own characteristics, is incompatible with the fundamental principles of the Charter of the United Nations and the Universal Declaration of Human Rights.

Article 3

For the purpose of realizing the conditions of full equality and all-round development of minorities, *as collectivities*, and members of minorities, it is essential to undertake measures which will enable them freely to express their characteristics, develop their culture, education, language, traditions and customs and to participate on an equitable basis in cultural, social, economic and political life of the country in which they live.

Article 4

1. In ensuring and promoting the rights of minorities strict respect for sovereignty, territorial integrity, political independence and non-interference in the internal affairs of countries in which minorities live, should be observed .

2. Respect for the aforementioned principles shall not prevent the

fulfilment of international commitments of States Members of the United Nations in relation to the minorities. Member States should fulfil, in good faith, their international commitments assumed under the Charter of the United Nations and international instruments, and the commitments assumed under other treaties or agreements to which they are parties.

Article 5

1. The development of contacts and co-operation among States, the exchange of information and experiences on the achievements of minorities in cultural, educational and other fields, creates favourable conditions for the promotion of the rights of minorities and for their general progress.

2. The States Members of the United Nations are invited to take the needs of minorities into account, in developing their co-operation with other states, especially in the fields of culture, education and related areas of particular importance for the minorities.

UNITED NATIONS

ECONOMIC AND SOCIAL COUNCIL

COMMISSION ON HUMAN RIGHTS

MARCH 5, 1990

Annex I

TEXT OF THE DRAFT DECLARATION AS ADOPTED IN
FIRST READING

Draft declaration on the rights of persons belonging to
national or ethnic, religious or linguistic minorities

The General Assembly,

Reaffirming that one of the basic aims of the United
Nations, as proclaimed in its Charter, is to promote and encourage respect
for human rights and for fundamental freedoms for all, without distinction as
to race, sex, language or religion,

[Reaffirming] [Reiterating] [Declaring] faith in
fundamental human rights, in the dignity and worth of the human person, in
the equal rights of men and women and of nations large and small,

Desiring to promote the realization of the principles
[concerning the rights of] [persons belonging to] [minorities] which form
the basis of the Charter of the United Nations, the Universal Declaration of
Human Rights, the Convention on the Prevention and Punishment of the
Crime of Genocide and the International Convention on the Elimination of
All Forms of Racial Discrimination as well as other relevant international
instruments [that have been adopted at the universal or regional level and
those concluded between individual States Members of the United Nations],

Inspired by [Based on] the provisions of article 27 of
the International Covenant on Civil and Political Rights concerning the
rights of persons belonging to ethnic, religious or linguistic minorities,

Considering that the promotion and protection of the
rights of persons belonging to [national or] ethnic, religious or linguistic
minorities contribute to the political and social stability of States in which

they live,

Confirming that friendly relations and co-operation among States, which take place in the spirit of the Declaration on Principles of International Law concerning Friendly Relations and Co-operation among States in accordance with the Charter of the United Nations, contribute to international peace and security and to the creation of more favourable conditions for the realization and promotion of human rights, including the rights of [persons belonging to] [national or], ethnic, linguistic and religious minorities,

Emphasizing that the constant promotion and realization of the rights of persons belonging to minorities, as an integral part of the development of society as a whole and within the constitutional framework, would in turn contribute to the strengthening of friendship and co-operation among peoples and States,

Bearing in mind the work done so far within the United Nations system, in particular the Commission on Human Rights, the Sub-Commission on Prevention of Discrimination and Protection of Minorities as well as the bodies established pursuant to the International Covenants on Human Rights and other relevant international human rights instruments on promoting and protecting the rights of persons belonging to [national or] ethnic, religious or linguistic minorities,

Recognizing the need to ensure even more effective implementation of international human rights instruments relating to the rights of persons belonging to [national or] ethnic, religious or linguistic minorities,

Proclaim this Declaration on the Rights of Persons Belonging to [National or] Ethnic, Religious or Linguistic Minorities:

Article 1

1.   [Persons belonging to] [national or] ethnic, linguistic and religious minorities (hereinafter referred to as minorities) have the right to respect for, and the promotion of, their ethnic, cultural, linguistic and religious identity without any discrimination.

2.   [Persons belonging to] minorities have the right to life, liberty and security of person and all other human rights and freedoms without discrimination.

84

Article 2

1.   In accordance with the Charter of the United Nations and other relevant international instruments, [persons belonging to] minorities have the right to be protected against any activity, including propaganda, [directed against minorities] which:

(i)   may threaten their existence [or identity];

(ii)   [interferes with their freedom of expression or association] [or the development of their own characteristics]; or

(iii)   otherwise prevents their full enjoyment and exercise of universally recognized human rights and fundamental freedoms.

2.   In accordance with their respective constitutional processes [and in accordance with the relevant international treaties to which they are parties], all States shall undertake to adopt legislative or other appropriate measures to prevent and combat such activities, with due regard to the principles embodied in this Declaration and in the Universal Declaration of Human Rights.

Article 3

1.   [Persons belonging to] minorities have the right, individually or in community with the other members of their group, to enjoy their own culture, to profess and practice their own religion, and to use their own language, freely and without interference or any form of discrimination.

2.   All States [which have not yet done so] shall [take measures to create favourable conditions to enable [persons belonging to] minorities to freely] / [ensure that [persons belonging to] minorities are freely able to] express their characteristics, to develop their [education,] culture, language, religion, traditions and customs, and to participate on an equitable basis in the cultural, religious, social, economic and political life in the country where they live.

3.   To the same ends, persons belonging to minorities shall enjoy, without any discrimination, the right to establish and maintain contacts with other members of their group [and with other minorities], especially by exercise of residence within the borders of each State, and the right to leave any country, including their own, and to return to their

countries. [This right shall be exercised in accordance with national legislation and relevant international human rights instruments.]

Article 4

1.   All States shall take legislative or other appropriate and effective measures, especially in the fields of teaching, education, culture and information, to promote and protect the human rights and fundamental freedoms of [persons belonging to] minorities.

2.   Such measures shall include facilitation of the enjoyment by [persons belonging to] minorities of their freedom to seek, receive and impart information and ideas of all kinds, regardless of frontiers, in particular through utilization of all forms of communication. [This freedom shall be exercised in accordance with national legislation and relevant international human rights instruments.]

3.   Such measures should also include the exchange of information [and experience] among States in the aforementioned fields, with a view to strengthening mutual understanding, tolerance and friendship among all people, including [persons belonging to] minorities, [as well as to develop further friendly relations and co-operation among States in accordance with the Charter of the United Nations.]/[as well as to develop further international co-operation in the spirit of the Declaration on Principles of International Law concerning Friendly Relations and Co-operation among States in accordance with the Charter of the United Nations.]

Article 5

1.   Nothing in this Declaration shall prevent the fulfilment of international obligations of States in relation to [persons belonging to] minorities. In particular, States shall fulfil in good faith the obligations and commitments they have assumed under international treaties and agreements to which they are parties.

2.   This Declaration shall not prejudice the enjoyment by all persons of universally recognized human rights and fundamental freedoms.

3.   Nothing in the present Declaration may be construed as permitting any activity contrary to the purposes and principles of the United Nations and, in particular, contrary to the sovereignty, territorial integrity and political independence of States.

86

4. In exercising their rights [persons belonging to] minorities shall respect the universally recognized human rights and fundamental freedoms of others.

Article 6

Member States of the United Nations shall endeavour, depending on their specific conditions, to create favourable political, educational, cultural and other conditions and to adopt adequate measures for the protection and promotion of the rights of minorities proclaimed in this Declaration.]

Article 7

(a) [Persons belonging to] [national,] ethnic, religious or linguistic minorities have the right to preserve their identity, and to participate effectively in the affairs of the State, and in decisions concerning the regions in which they live [through national institutions and, where possible, regional institutions].

(b) National policies and programmes, as well as programmes of international co-operation and assistance, shall be planned and implemented with due regard for their legitimate interests.

Article 8

The organs and specified agencies of the United Nations system shall contribute to the full realization of the rights and principles set forth in this Declaration, within their respective fields of competence.

New article

This Declaration shall be carried out in a spirit of mutual understanding, tolerance, [good neighbourliness] and friendship among States and [all peoples]/[peoples] and [national], racial, ethnic, religious and linguistic groups in conformity with the purposes and principles of the United Nations.

To be included within a resolution accompanying the Declaration

(i) The Secretary-General shall organize regional and global technical meetings to stimulate an exchange of experience in this field among governments and with the people affected by this Declaration;

(ii)   The Sub-Commission on the Prevention of Discrimination and Protection of Minorities shall undertake annually a review of the national and international measures which have been taken for the implementation of this Declaration, and report on the problems encountered and progress achieved;

(iii)   States shall provide, as far as possible, information on the identity, numbers, location, organization, and social and economic characteristics of minorities in their reports to bodies established under United Nations conventions in the field of human rights;

(iv)   United Nations organs and specialized agencies shall give special consideration to requests for technical co-operation and assistance that are designed to achieve the aims of this Declaration.

Annex II

TEXT OF THE DRAFT DECLARATION
AS ADOPTED IN SECOND READING

Draft declaration on the rights of persons belonging to national or ethnic, religious and linguistic minorities

The General Assembly,

Reaffirming that one of the basic aims of the United Nations, as proclaimed in its Charter, is to promote and encourage respect for human rights and for fundamental freedoms for all, without distinction as to race, sex, language or religion,

Reaffirming faith in fundamental human rights, in the dignity and worth of the human person, in the equal rights of men and women and of nations large and small,

Desiring to promote the realization of the principles contained in the Charter of the United Nations, the Universal Declaration of Human Rights, the Convention on the Prevention and Punishment of the Crime of Genocide, the International Convention on the Elimination of All Forms of Racial Discrimination, the International Covenant on Civil and Political Rights, the International Covenant on Economic, Social and Cultural Rights, the Declaration on the Elimination of All Forms of Intolerance and of Discrimination Based on Religion or Belief, and the Convention on the Rights of the Child, as well as other relevant international instruments that have been adopted at the universal or regional level and those concluded between individual States Members of the United Nations,

Inspired by the provisions of article 27 of the International Covenant on Civil and Political Rights concerning the rights of persons belonging to ethnic, religious or linguistic minorities,

Considering that the promotion and protection of the rights of persons belonging to national or ethnic, religious and linguistic minorities contribute to the political and social stability of States in which they live,

Emphasizing that the constant promotion and realization of the rights of persons belonging to national or ethnic, religious and linguistic minorities, as an integral part of the development of society as a whole and within a democratic framework based on the rule of law, would contribute to the strengthening of friendship and cooperation among peoples and States,

Considering that the United Nations has an important role to play regarding the protection of minorities,

Bearing in mind the work done so far within the United Nations system, in particular the Commission on Human Rights, the Sub-Commission on Prevention of Discrimination and Protection of Minorities as well as the bodies established pursuant to the International Covenants on Human Rights and other relevant international human rights instruments on promoting and protecting the rights of persons belonging to national or ethnic, religious and linguistic minorities,

Taking into account the important work which is carried out by intergovernmental and non-governmental organisations in protecting minorities and in promoting and protecting the rights of persons belonging to national or ethnic, religious and linguistic minorities,

Recognizing the need to ensure even more effective implementation of international instruments with regard to the rights of persons belonging to national or ethnic, religious and linguistic minorities,

Proclaims this Declaration on the Rights of Persons Belonging to National or Ethnic, Religious and Linguistic Minorities:

Article 1

1.   States shall protect the existence and the national or ethnic,

cultural, religious and linguistic identity of minorities within their respective territories, and shall encourage conditions for the promotion of that identity.

2. States shall adopt appropriate legislative and other measures to achieve those ends.

Article 2

1. Persons belonging to national or ethnic, religious and linguistic minorities (hereinafter referred to as persons belonging to minorities) have the right to enjoy their own culture, to profess and practise their own religion, and to use their own language, in private and in public, freely and without interference or any form of discrimination.

2. Persons belonging to minorities have the right to participate effectively in cultural, religious, social, economic and public life.

3. Persons belonging to minorities have the right to participate effectively in decisions on the national and, where appropriate, regional level concerning the minority to which they belong or the regions in which they live, in a manner not incompatible with national legislation.

4. Persons belonging to minorities have the right to establish and maintain their own associations.

5. Persons belonging to minorities have the right to establish and maintain, without any discrimination, free and peaceful contacts with other members of their group, with persons belonging to other minorities, as well as contacts across frontiers with citizens of other States to whom they are related by national or ethnic, religious or linguistic ties.

Article 3

1. Persons belonging to minorities may exercise their rights including those as set forth in this Declaration individually as well as in community with other members of their group, without any discrimination.

2. No disadvantage shall result for any person belonging to a minority as the consequence of the exercise or non-exercise of the rights as set forth in this Declaration.

Article 4

1. States shall take measures where required to ensure that persons

belonging to minorities may exercise fully and effectively all their human rights and fundamental freedoms without any discrimination and in full equality before the law.

2. States shall take measures to create favourable conditions to enable persons belonging to minorities to express their characteristics and to develop their culture, language, religion, traditions and customs, except where specific practices are in violation of national law and contrary to international standards.

3. States should take appropriate measures so that, wherever possible, persons belonging to minorities have adequate opportunities to learn their mother tongue or to have instruction in their mother tongue.

4. States should, where appropriate, take measures in the field of education, in order to encourage knowledge of the history, traditions, language and culture of the minorities existing within their territory. Persons belonging to minorities should have adequate opportunities to gain knowledge of the society as a whole.

5. States should consider appropriate measures so that persons belonging to minorities may participate fully in the economic progress and development in their country.

Article 5

1. National policies and programmes shall be planned and implemented with due regard for the legitimate interests of persons belonging to minorities.

2. Programmes of cooperation and assistance among States should be planned and implemented with due regard for the legitimate interests of persons belonging to minorities.

Article 6

States should cooperate on questions relating to persons belonging to minorities, including exchange of information and experiences, in order to promote mutual understanding and confidence.

Article 7

States should cooperate in order to promote respect for the

rights as set forth in this Declaration.

Article 8

1. Nothing in this Declaration shall prevent the fulfilment of international obligations of States in relation to persons belonging to minorities. In particular, States shall fulfil in good faith the obligations and commitments they have assumed under international treaties and agreements to which they are parties.

2. The exercise of the rights as set forth in this Declaration shall not prejudice the enjoyment by all persons of universally recognized human rights and fundamental freedoms.

3. Measures taken by States in order to ensure the effective enjoyment of the rights as set forth in this Declaration shall not *prima facie* be considered contrary to the principle of equality contained in the Universal Declaration of Human Rights.

4. Nothing in this Declaration may be construed as permitting any activity contrary to the purposes and principles of the United Nations, including sovereign equality, territorial integrity and political independence of States.

Article 9

The organs and specialized agencies of the United Nations system shall contribute to the full realization of the rights and principles as set forth in this Declaration, within their respective fields of competence.

****

[Date of adoption by the U.N. General Assembly: Dec. 18, 1992]

Council of Europe

European Commission   for Democracy through Law

Commission europeenne pour la democratie par le droit
******

PROPOSAL FOR A EUROPEAN CONVENTION
FOR THE PROTECTION OF   MINORITIES

(Adopted during the 6th meeting, on 8 February 1991)

PREAMBLE

The member States of the Council of Europe and the other States, signatory hereto,

Considering that the aim of the Council of Europe is to achieve greater unity between its members, for the purpose of safeguarding and realising the ideals and principles which are their common heritage;

Considering that the dignity and equal worth of every human being constitute fundamental elements of these principles;

Considering that minorities exist in member States of the Council of Europe and in Central and Eastern European States;

Considering that minorities contribute to the pluriformity and cultural diversity within European States;

Having regard to the work carried out within the CSCE and in particular to the Declaration adopted during the Copenhagen meeting in June 1990, as well as the Charter of Paris for a new Europe, of 21 November 1990;

Having regard to Article 14 of the Convention for the Protection of Human

Rights and Fundamental Freedoms and to Article 27 of the International Covenant on Civil and Political Rights;

Considering that an adequate solution to the problem of minorities in Europe is an essential factor for democracy, justice, stability and peace;

Being resolved to implement an effective protection of the rights of minorities and of persons belonging to those minorities,

Have agreed as follows :

CHAPTER I - GENERAL PRINCIPLES

Article 1

1. The international protection of the rights of ethnic, linguistic and religious minorities, as well as the rights of individuals belonging to those minorities, as guaranteed by the present Convention, is a fundamental component of the international protection of Human Rights, and as such falls within the scope of international co-operation.

2. It does not permit any activity which is contrary to the fundamental principles of international law and in particular of sovereignty, territorial integrity and political independence of States.

3. It must be carried out in good faith, in a spirit of understanding, tolerance and good neighbourliness between States.

Article 2

1. For the purposes of this Convention, the term "minority" shall mean a group which is smaller in number than the rest of the population of a State, whose members, who are nationals of that State, have ethnical, religious or linguistic features different from those of the rest of the population, and are guided by the will to safeguard their culture, traditions, religion or language.

2. Any group coming within the terms of this definition shall be treated as an ethnic, religious or linguistic minority.
3. To belong to a [national] minority shall be a matter of individual choice and no disadvantage may arise from the exercise of such choice.

94

CHAPTER II - RIGHTS AND OBLIGATIONS

Article 3

1. Minorities shall have the right to be protected against any activity capable of threatening their existence.

2. They shall have the right to the respect, safeguard and development of their ethnical, religious, or linguistic identity.

Article 4

1. Any person belonging to a minority shall have the right to enjoy the same rights as any other citizen, without distinction and on an equal footing.

2. The adoption of special measures in favour of minorities or of individuals belonging to minorities and aimed at promoting equality between them and the rest of the population or at taking due account of their specific conditions shall not be considered as an act of discrimination.

Article 5

With a view to promoting and reinforcing their common features, persons belonging to a minority shall have the right to associate and to maintain contacts, in particular with other members of their group, including across national borders. This right shall include notably the right to leave freely one's country and to go back to it.

Article 6

1. Persons belonging to a minority shall have the right to freely preserve, express and develop their cultural identity in all its aspects, free of any attempts at assimilation against their will.

2. In particular, they shall have the right to express themselves, to receive and to issue information and ideas through means of communication of their own.

Article 7

Any person belonging to a linguistic minority shall have the right to use his language freely, in public as well as in private.

Article 8

Whenever a minority reaches a substantial percentage of the population of a region or of the total population, its members shall have the right, as far as possible, to speak and write in their own language to the political, administrative and judicial authorities of this region or, where appropriate, of the State. These authorities shall have a corresponding obligation.

Article 9

Whenever the conditions of article 8 are fulfilled, in State schools, obligatory schooling shall include, for pupils belonging to the minority, study of their mother tongue. As far as possible, all or part of the schooling shall be given in the mother tongue of pupils belonging to the minority. However, should the State not be in a position to provide such schooling, it must permit children who so wish to attend private schools. In such a case, the State shall have the right to prescribe that the official language or languages also be taught in such schools.

Article 10

Any person belonging to a religious minority shall have the right to manifest his religion or belief, either alone or in community with others and in public or private, in worship, teaching, practice or observance.

Article 11

Any person belonging to a minority whose rights set forth in the present Convention are violated shall have an effective remedy before a national authority.

Article 12

The rights set forth in Articles 5, 7 and 10 of this Convention shall be subject only to such limitations as are prescribed by law and are necessary in a democratic society in the interests of public safety, for the protection of public order, health or morals, or for the protection of the rights and freedoms of others.

Article 13

States shall refrain from pursuing or encouraging policies aimed at the assimilation of minorities or aimed at intertionally modifying the proportions of the population in the regions inhabited by minorities.

Article 14

1.   States shall favour the effective participation of minorities in public affairs in particular in decisions affecting the regions where they live or in the matters affecting them.

2.   As far as possible, States shall take minorities into account when dividing the national territory into political and administrative sub-divisions, as well as into constituencies.

Article 15

1.   Any person who belongs to a minority shall loyally fulfil the obligations deriving from his status as a national of his State.

2.   In the exercise of the rights set forth in this Convention, any person who belongs to a minority shall respect the national legislation, the rights of others, in particular those of the members of the majority and of other minorities.

Article 16

States shall take the necessary measures with a view to ensuring that, in any region where those who belong to a minority represent the majority of the population, those who do not belong to this minority shall not suffer from any discrimination.

Article 17

This Convention shall not prejudice the provisions of domestic law or international agreement which provide greater protection for minorities or persons belonging to minorities.

CHAPTER III - CONTROL MACHINERY

Article 18

To ensure the observance of the undertakings by the Parties in the present Convention, there shall be set up a European Committee for the Protection of Minorities (hereinafter referred to as "the Committee").

Article 21

1. The Committee shall meet in camera.
2. A quorum shall be equal to the majority of its members. The decisions of the Committee stall be taken by a majority of the members present.

Article 22

1. The Committee shall meet as the circumstances require, at least once a year. The meetings shall be convened by the Secretary General of the Council of Europe.
2. The Committee shall draw up its own Rules of Procedure.
3. The Secretariat of the Committee shall be provided by the Secretary General of the Council of Europe.

Article 23

1. In the application of this Convention, the Committee and the competent national authorities of the Party concerned shall co-operate with each other.
2. Parties shall provide the Committee with the facilities necessary to carry out its tasks, in particular access to their territories, and the right to travel without restriction and to communicate freely with any person from whom it believes it can obtain relevant information.

Article 24

1. The Parties shall submit to the Committee, through the Secretary General of the Council of Europe, reports on the measures they have adopted to give effect to their undertakings under this Convention, within one year of the entry into force of the Convention for the Party concerned. The Parties shall submit supplementary reports at three yearly intervals concerning any new measure adopted, as well as any other report requested

by the Committee.

2.   Those reports shall be examined by the Committee who will forward them to the Committee of Ministers of the Council of Europe with its observations.

3.   By the majority of two-thirds of the members entitled to sit on the Committee, the Committee may make any necessary recommendations to a Party.

Article 25

1.   Provided that a Party has, by declaration addressed to the Secretary General of the Council of Europe, recognised the competence of the Committee to receive a State's request, the Committee may receive petitions from any Party which considers that another Party does not respect the provisions of this Convention.

2.   The declarations provided for in paragraph 1 may be made for a specific period. In this case, they shall be renewed automatically for the same period, unless withdrawn by previous notice of one year before the expiration of the period of validity.

3.   The Committee shall only exercise the powers provided for in this Article when at least five Parties are bound by declarations made in accordance with paragraph 1.

Article 26

1.   Provided that a Party has, by declaration addressed to the Secretary General of the Council of Europe, recognised the competence of the Committee to receive individual petitions, it may receive such petitions from any person, group of individuals or any international non-governmental organisation representative of minorities, claiming to be the victim of a violation by this Party of the rights set forth in this Convention.

2.   The declarations provided for in paragraph 1 may be made for a specific period. In this case, they shall be renewed automatically for the same period, unless withdrawn by previous notice of one year before the expiration of the period of validity.

3. The Parties who have made the declaration provided for in paragraph 1 undertake not to hinder in any way the effective exercise of the right of individual petition.

4. The Committee shall only exercise the powers provided for in this Article when at least five Parties are bound by declarations made in accordance with paragraph 1.

Article 27

1. The Committee may only deal with the matter referred to it under Article 26 after all domestic remedies have been exhausted, according to the generally recognised rules of international law.

2. The Committee shall declare inadmissible petitions submitted under Article 26 which :

a. are anonymous;

b. are substantially the same as a matter which has already been examined by the Committee;

c. have already been submitted to another international body and do not contain any relevant new information;

d. are incompatible with the Provisions of this Convention, manifestly ill-founded or, an abuse of the right of petition;

e. are submitted to the Committee more than six months from the final internal decision.

Article 28

In the event of the Committee accepting a petition referred to it:
a. it shall, with the view to ascertaining the facts, undertake together with the representatives of the parties an examination of the petition and, if need be, an investigation.
b. it endeavours to reach a friendly settlement of the matter on the basis of respect of this Convention. If it succeeds it shall draw up a report which shall contain a statement of the facts and of the solution reached and be sent to the State or States concerned.

Article 29

1.   If no friendly settlement has been reached, the Committee shall draw up a report as to whether the facts found disclose a breach by the State concerned of its obligations under this Convention and make such proposals as it thinks are necessary.

2.   The report shall be transmitted to the Committee of Ministers, to the State or States concerned and to the Secretary General of the Council of Europe.

3.   The Committee of Ministers may take any follow-up action it thinks fit in order to ensure respect of the Convention.

Article 30

This Convention shall not be construed as limiting or derogating from the competence of the organs of the European Convention on Human Rights or from the obligations assumed by the Parties under that Convention.

CHAPTER IV - AMENDMENTS
TO THE ARTICLES OF THE CONVENTION

Article 31

1.   Amendments to the Articles of this Convention may be proposed by a Party or by the Committee of Ministers of the Council of Europe.

2.   Any proposal for amendment shall be communicated by the Secretary General of the Council of Europe to the States mentioned in Article 32 and to every State which has acceded to or has been invited to accede to this Convention, in accordance with the provisions of Article 34.

3.   Any amendment proposed by a Party or the Committee of Ministers shall be communicated to the Committee which shall submit to the Committee of Ministers its opinion on the proposed amendment.

4.   The Committee of Ministers shall consider the proposed amendment and the opinion submitted by the Committee and may adopt the amendment,

after having consulted the non-member States Parties to the Convention.

5.   The text of any amendment adopted by the Committee of Ministers in accordance with paragraph 4 of this Article shall be forwarded to the Parties for acceptance.

6.   Any amendment adopted in accordance with paragraph 4 of this Article shall come into force on the first day of the month following the expiration of a period of one month after all Parties have informed the Secretary General of their acceptance thereof.

CHAPTER V - FINAL PROVISIONS

Article 32

1.   This Convention shall be open for signature by member States of the Council of Europe and non-member States which have participated in its elaboration.   It is subject to ratification, acceptance or approval. Instruments of ratification, acceptance or approval shall be deposited with the Secretary General of the Council of Europe.

Article 33

1.   The Convention shall enter into force on the first day of the month following the expiration of a period of one month after the date on which five States, including at least four member States of the Council of Europe, have expressed their consent to be bound by the Convention in accordance with the provisions of Article 32.

2.   In respect of any signatory State which subsequently expresses its consent to be bound by it, the Convention shall enter into force on the first day of the month following the expiration of a period of one month after the date of signature or of the deposit of the instrument of ratification, acceptance or approval.

Article 34

1.   After the entry into force of this Convention, the Committee of Ministers of the Council of Europe, after consulting the Parties, may invite to accede to the Convention any European non-member State by a decision

taken by the majority provided for in Article 20 d. of the Statute of the Council of Europe and by the unanimous vote of the representatives of the Contracting States entitled to sit on the Committee of Ministers.

In respect of any acceding State, the Convention shall enter into force on the first day of the month following the expiration of a period of one month after the date of the deposit of the instrument of accession with the Secretary General of the Council of Europe.

Article 35

1. Any State may, at the time of signature or when depositing the instrument of ratification, acceptance, approval or accession, specify the territory or territories to which this Convention shall apply.

2. Any State may, at any later date, by a declaration addressed to the Secretary General, extend the application of this Convention to any other territory specified in the declaration. In respect of such territory the Convention shall enter into force on the first day of the month following the expiration of a period of one month after the date of receipt of such declaration by the Secretary General.

3, Any declaration made under the two preceding paragraphs may, in respect of any territory mentioned in such declaration, be withdrawn by a notification addressed to the Secretary General. Such withdrawal shall become effective on the first day of the month following the expiration of a period of six months after the date of receipt of the notification by the Secretary General.

Article 36

1. Any Party may, at any time, denounce this Convention by means of a notification addressed to the Secretary General of the Council of Europe.

2. Such denunciation shall become effective on the first day of the month following the expiration of a period of six months after the date of receipt of the notification by the Secretary General.

Article 37

the Secretary General of the Council of Europe shall notify the Parties, the other member States of the Council of Europe, the non-member States which have participated in the elaboration of this Convention and any State which has acceded or has been invited to accede to it of:

a. any signature in accordance with Article 32;

b. the deposit of any instrument of ratification, acceptance, or accession in accordance with Article 32 of 34;

c. any date of entry into force of this Convention in accordance with Articles 33 and 34;

d. any declaration made under the provisions of Articles 25 and 26;

e. any report prepared in pursuance of the provisions of Article 24;

f. any proposal for amendment or any amendment adopted in accordance with Article 31 and the date on which the amendment comes into force;

g. any declaration made under the provisions of Article 35;

h. any notification made under the provisions of Article 36 and the date on which the denunciation takes effect;

i. any other act, notification or communication relating to this Convention.

In witness whereof the undersigned, being duly authorised thereto, have signed this Convention.

Done at ....., the ....in English and French, both texts being equally authentic, in a single copy which shall be deposited in the archives of the Council of Europe. The Secretary General of the Council of Europe shall transmit certified copies to each member State of the Council of Europe, to the non-member States which have participated in the elaboration of this Convention and to any State invited to accede to it.

NOTE: This proposal **was not adopted by the Council of Europe.**

EREC1201.WP
1403-1/2/93-17-E

Provisional edition

RECOMMENDATION 1201 (1993)1

on an additional protocol on the rights of minorities
to the European Convention on Human Rights

[Assembly debate on 1 February 1993 (22nd sitting). See Doc. 6742, report of
the Committee on Legal Affairs and Human Rights (Rapporteur: Mr Worms) and
Doc. 6749, opinion of the Political Affairs Committee (Rapporteur: Mr de Puig).
Text adopted by the Assembly on 1 February 1993 (22nd sitting)].

1.   The Assembly recalls its Recommendations 1134 (1990) and 1177
(1992) and its Orders No.456 (1990) and No.474 (1992) on the rights of
minorities. In the texts adopted on 5 February 1992 it asked the Committee
of Ministers to:
i. conclude as soon as possible the work under way for the elaboration of a
charter for regional or minority languages and do its utmost to ensure the
rapid implementation of the charter;

ii. draw up an additional protocol on the rights of minorities to the
European Convention on Human Rights;

iii provide the Council of Europe with a suitable mediation instrument.

2.   By adopting the European Charter for Regional or Minority Languages
- a Council of Europe Convention - on 22 June 1992, the Committee of
Ministers gave the Assembly satisfaction on the first point. The charter, on
which legislation in our member states will have to be based, will also be

able to give guidance to many other states on a difficult and sensitive subject.

3. There remains the rapid implementation of the charter. It is encouraging that when it was opened for signature on 5 November 1992, eleven Council of Europe member states signed it straight away. But one has to go further.

4. The Assembly therefore appeals to member states which have not yet signed the Charter to do so and to urge all of them to ratify it speedily, accepting as many of its clauses as possible.

5. The Assembly reserves the right to return, at a later date, to the question of a suitable mediation instrument of the Council of Europe which it already proposed to set.

6. It has been advised of the terms of reference given by the Committee of Ministers to the Steering Committee for Human Rights and its Committee of Experts for the Protection of National Minorities and wishes to give its full support to this work and actively promote it.

7. Through the inclusion in the European Convention on Human Rights of certain rights of persons belonging to minorities as well as organisations entitled to represent them, such persons could benefit from the remedies offered by the convention, particularly the right to submit applications to the European Commission and Court of Human Rights.

8. Consequently the Assembly recommends that the Committee of Ministers adopt an additional protocol on the rights of national minorities to the European Convention on Human Rights, drawing on the text reproduced below, which is an integral part of this recommendation .

9. As this matter is extremely urgent and one of the most important activities currently under way at the Council of Europe, the Assembly also recommends that the Committee of Ministers speed up its work schedule so that the meeting of Heads of State and Government (Vienna, 8 and 9 October 1993) will be able to adopt a protocol on the rights of minorities and open it for signature on that occasion.

Rec. 1201

TEXT OF THE PROPOSAL FOR AN ADDITIONAL PROTOCOL TO THE CONVENTION FOR THE PROTECTION OF HUMAN RIGHTS AND FUNDAMENTAL FREEDOMS, CONCERNING PERSONS BELONGING TO NATIONAL MINORITIES

Preamble

The member states of the Council of Europe signatory hereto;

1. Considering that the diversity of peoples and cultures with which it is imbued is one of the main sources of the richness and vitality of European civilisation,

2. Considering the important contribution of national minorities to the cultural diversity and dynamism of the states of Europe;

3. Considering that only the recognition of the rights of persons belonging to a national minority within a state and the international protection of those rights are capable of putting a lasting end to ethnic confrontations, and thus of helping to guarantee justice, democracy, stability and peace;

4. Considering that the rights concerned are those which any person may exercise either singly or jointly;

5. Considering that the international protection of the rights of minorities is an essential aspect of the international protection of human rights and, as such, a domain for international co-operation,
Have agreed as follows:

Section I: Definition

Article 1
For the purposes of this convention [1 The term "convention" in this text refers to the European Convention for the Protection of Human Rights and Fundamental Freedoms]. the expression "national minority" refers to a group of persons in a state who
a. reside on the territory on that state and are citizens thereof,

b. maintain long standing, firm and lasting ties with that state,

c. display distinctive ethnic, cultural, religious or linguistic characteristics,

d. are sufficiently representative, although smaller in number than the rest of the population of that state or of a region of that state,

e. are motivated by a concern to preserve together that which constitutes theircommon identity, including their culture, their traditions, their religion or their language.

Section 2: General principles

Article 2

1. Membership of a national minority shall be a matter of free personal choice.

2. No disadvantage shall result from the choice or the renunciation of such membership.

Article 3

1. Every person belonging to a national minority shall have the right to express, preserve and develop in complete freedom his/her religious, ethnic, linguistic or cultural identity, without being subjected to any attempt at assimilation against his/her will.

2. Every person belonging to a national minority may exercise his/her rights and enjoy them individually or in association with others.

Article 4

All persons belonging to a national minority shall be equal before the law. Any discrimination based on membership of a national minority shall be prohibited.

Article 5

Deliberate changes to the demographic composition of the region in which a national minority is settled, to the detriment of that minority, shall be prohibited.

Section 3: Substantive rights

Article 6

All persons belonging to a national minority shall have the right to set up their own organisations, including political parties.

Article 7

1. Every person belonging to a national minority shall have the right freely to use his/her mother tongue in private and in public, both orally and in writing. This right shall also apply to the use of his/her language in publications and in the audiovisual sector.

2. Every person belonging to a national minority shall have the right to use his/her surname and first names in his/her mother tongue and to official recognition of his/her surname and first names.

3. In the regions in which substantial numbers of a national minority are settled, the persons belonging to a national minority shall have the right to use their mother tongue in their contacts with the administrative authorities and in proceedings before the courts and legal authorities.

4. In the regions in which substantial numbers of a national minority are settled, the persons belonging to that minority shall have the right to display in their language local names, signs, inscriptions and other similar information visible to the public. This does not deprive the authorities of their right to display the above-mentioned information in the official language or languages of the state.

Article 8

1. Every person belonging to a national minority shall have the right to learn his/her mother tongue and to receive an education in his/her mother tongue at an appropriate number of schools and of state educational and training establishments, located in accordance with the geographical distribution of the minority.
2. The persons belonging to a national minority shall have the right to set up and manage their own schools and educational and training

establishments within the framework of the legal system of the state.

Article 9

If a violation of the rights protected by this protocol is alleged, every person belonging to a national minority or any representative organisation shall have an effective remedy before a state authority.

Article 10

Every person belonging to a national minority, while duly respecting the territorial integrity of the state, shall have the right to have free and unimpeded contacts with the citizens of another country with whom this minority shares ethnic, religious or linguistic features or a cultural identity.

Article 11

In the regions where they are in a majority the persons belonging to a national minority shall have the right to have at their disposal appropriate local or autonomous authorities or to have a special status, matching the specific historical and territorial situation and in accordance with the domestic legislation of the state.

Section 4: Implementation of the protocol

Article 12

1. Nothing in this protocol may be construed as limiting or restricting an individual right of persons belonging to a national minority or a collective right of a national minority embodied in the legislation of the Contracting State or in an international agreement to which that state is a party.

2. Measures taken for the sole purpose of protecting ethnic groups, fostering their appropriate development and ensuring that they are granted equal rights and treatment with respect to the rest of the population in the administrative, political, economic, social and cultural fields and in other spheres shall not be considered as discrimination.

Article 13

The exercise of the rights and freedoms listed in this protocol fully apply to the persons belonging to the majority in the whole of the state but which constitute a minority in one or several of its regions.

Article 14

The exercise of the rights and freedoms set forth in this protocol are not meant to restrict the duties and responsibilities of the citizens of the state. However, this exercise may only be made subject to such formalities, conditions, restrictions or penalties as are prescribed by law and necessary in a democratic society in the interests of national security, territorial integrity or public safety, for the prevention of disorder or crime, for the protection of health and morals and for the protection of the rights and freedoms of others.

Section 5: Final clauses

Article 15

No derogation under Article 15 of the convention from the provisions of this protocol shall be allowed, save in respect of its Article 10.

Article 16

No reservation may be made under Article 64 of the convention in respect of the provisions of this protocol.

Article 17

The States Parties shall regard the provisions of Articles 1 to 11 of this protocol as additional articles of the convention and all the provisions of the convention shall apply accordingly.

Article 18

This protocol shall be open for signature by the member states of the Council of Europe which are signatories to the convention. It shall be subject to ratification, acceptance or approval. A member state of the Council of Europe may not ratify, accept or approve this protocol unless it simultaneously ratifies or has previously ratified the convention. Instruments of ratification, acceptance or approval shall be deposited with the Secretary General of the Council of Europe.

Article 19

1. This protocol shall enter into force on the first day of the month following the date on which five member states of the Council of Europe have expressed their consent to be bound by the protocol in accordance with the provisions of Article 17.

2. In respect of any member state which subsequently expresses its consent to be bound by it, the protocol shall enter into force on the first day of the month following the date of the deposit of the instrument of ratification, acceptance or approval.

Article 20

The Secretary General of the Council of Europe shall notify the member states of the Council of:

a. any signature;
b. the deposit of any instrument of ratification, acceptance or approval;
c. any date of entry into force of this protocol;

any other act, notification or communication relating to this protocol.

In witness whereof the undersigned, being duly authorised thereto, have signed this protocol.

Done at Strasbourg on ....
in English and French, both texts being equally authentic, in a single copy, which shall be deposited in the archives of the Council of Europe. The Secretary General of the Council of Europe shall transmit certified copies to each member state of the Council of Europe.

[NOTE: The proposal for the Additional Protocol **was not adopted**.]

FRAMEWORK CONVENTION
FOR THE PROTECTION
OF NATIONAL MINORITIES

The member States of the Council of Europe and the other States, signatories to the present framework Convention,

Considering that the aim of the Council of Europe is to achieve greater unity between its members for the purpose of safeguarding and realising the ideals and principles which are their common heritage;

Considering that one of the methods by which that aim is to be pursued is the maintenance and further realisation of human rights and fundamental freedoms;

Wishing to follow-up the Declaration of the Heads of State and Governrnent of the member States of the Council of Europe adopted in Vienna on 9 October 1993;

Being resolved to protect within their respective territories the existence of national minorities;

Considering that the upheavals of European history have shown that the protection of national minorities is essential to stability, democratic security and peace in this continent;

Considering that a pluralist and genuinely democratic society should not only respect the ethnic, cultural, linguistic and religious identity of each person belonging to a national minority, but also create appropriate conditions enabling them to express, preserve and develop this identity;

Considering that the creation of a climate of tolerance and dialogue is necessary to enable cultural diversity to be a source and a factor, not of division, but of enrichment for each society;

Considering that the realisation of a tolerant and prosperous Europe does not depend solely on co-operation between States but also requires transfrontier co-operation between local and regional authorities without prejudice to the constitution and territorial integrity of each State;

Having regard to the Convention for the Protection of Human Rights and Fundamental Freedoms and the Protocols thereto;

Having regard to the commitments concerning the protection of national minorities in United Nations conventions and declarations and in the documents of the Conference on Security and Co-operation in Europe, particularly the Copenhagen Document of 29 June 1990;

Being resolved to define the principles to be respected and the obligations which flow from them, in order to ensure, in the member States and such other States as may become Parties to the present instrument, the effective protection of national minorities and of the rights and freedoms of persons belonging to those minorities, within the rule of law, respecting the territorial integrity and national sovereignty of states;

Being determined to implement the principles set out in this framework Convention through national legislation and appropriate governmental policies,

Have agreed as follows:

Section I

Article 1

The protection of national minorities and of the rights and freedoms of persons belonging to those minorities forms an integral part of the international protection of human rights, and as such falls within the scope of international co-operation.

Article 2

The provisions of this framework Convention shall be applied in good faith, in a spirit of understanding and tolerance and in conformity with the principles of good neighbourliness, friendly relations and co-operation between States.

Article 3

1. Every person belonging to a national minority shall have the right freely to choose to be treated or not to be treated as such and no disadvantage shall result from this choice or from the exercise of the rights which are connected to that choice.

2. Persons belonging to national minorities may exercise the rights and enjoy the freedoms flowing from the principles enshrined in the present framework Convention individually as well as in community with others.

Section II

Article 4

1. The Parties undertake to guarantee to persons belonging to national minorities the right of equality before the law and of equal protection of the law. In this respect, any discrimination based on belonging to a national minority shall be prohibited.

2. The Parties undertake to adopt, where necessary, adequate measures in order to promote, in all areas of economic, social, political and cultural life, full and effective equality between persons belonging to a national minority and those belonging to the majority. In this respect, they shall take due account of the specific conditions of the persons belonging to national minorities.

3. The measures adopted in accordance with paragraph 2 shall not be considered to be an act of discrimination.

Article 5

1. The Parties undertake to promote the conditions necessary for persons belonging to national minorities to maintain and develop their culture, and to preserve the essential elements of their identity, namely their religion, language, traditions and cultural heritage.

2. Without prejudice to measures taken in pursuance of their general integration policy, the Parties shall refrain from policies or practices aimed at assimilation of persons belonging to national minorities against their will and shall protect these persons from any action aimed at such assimilation.

Article 6

1. The Parties shall encourage a spirit of tolerance and intercultural dialogue and take effective measures to promote mutual respect and understanding and co-operation among all persons living on their territory, irrespective of those persons' ethnic, cultural, linguistic or religious identity, in particular in the fields of education, culture and the media.

2. The Parties undertake to take appropriate measures to protect persons who may be subject to threats or acts of discrimination, hostility or violence as a result of their ethnic, cultural, linguistic or religious identity.

Article 7

The Parties shall ensure respect for the right of every person belonging to a national minority to freedom of peaceful assembly, freedom of association, freedom of expression, and freedom of thought, conscience and religion.

Article 8

The Parties undertake to recognise that every person belonging to a national minority has the right to manifest his or her religion or belief and to establish religious institutions, organisations and associations.

Article 9

1. The Parties undertake to recognise that the right to freedom of expression of every person belonging to a national minority includes freedom to hold opinions and to receive and impart information and ideas in the minority language, without interference by public authorities and regardless of frontiers. The Parties shall ensure, within the framework of their legal systems, that persons belonging to a national minority are not discriminated against in their access to the media.

2. Paragraph 1 shall not prevent Parties from requiring the licensing, without discrimination and based on objective criteria, of sound radio and television broadcasting, or cinema enterprises.

3. The Parties shall not hinder the creation and the use of printed media by persons belonging to national minorities. In the legal framework of sound

radio and television broadcasting, they shall ensure, as far as possible, and taking into account the provisions of paragraph 1, that persons belonging to national minorities are granted the possibility of creating and using their own media.

4. In the framework of their legal systems, the Parties shall adopt adequate measures in order to facilitate access to the media for persons belonging to national minorities and in order to promote tolerance and permit cultural pluralism.

Article 10

1. The Parties undertake to recognise that everv person belonging to a national minority has the right to use freely and without interference his or her minority language, in private and in public, orally and in writing.

2. In areas inhabited by persons belonging to national minorities traditionally or in substantial numbers, if those persons so request and where such a request corresponds to a real need, the Parties shall endeavour to ensure, as far as possible, the conditions which would make it possible to use the minority language in relations between those persons and the administrative authorities.

3. The Parties undertake to guarantee the right of every person belonging to a national minority to be informed promptly, in a language which he or she understands, of the reasons for his or her arrest, and of the nature and cause of any accusation against him or her, and to defend himself or herself in this language, if necessary with the free assistance of an interpreter.

Article 11

1. The Parties undertake to recognise that every person belonging to a national minority has the right to use his or her surname (patronym) and first names in the minority language and the right to official recognition of them, according to modalities provided for in their legal system.

2. The Parties undertake to recognise that every person belonging to a national minority has the right to display in his or her minority language signs, inscriptions and other information of a private nature visible to the public.

3. In areas traditionally inhabited by substantial numbers of persons belonging to a national minority, the Parties shall endeavour, in the framework of their legal system, including, where appropriate, agreements with other States, and taking into account their specific conditions, to display traditional local names, street names and other topographical indications intended for the public also in the minority language when there is a sufficient demand for such indications.

Article 12

1. The Parties shall, where appropriate, take measures in the fields of education and research to foster knowledge of the culture, history, language and religion of their national minorities and of the majority.

2. In this context the Parties shall inter alia provide adequate opportunities for teacher training and access to textbooks, and facilitate contacts among students and teachers of different communities.

3. The Parties undertake to promote equal opportunities for access to education at all levels for persons belonging to national minorities.

Article 13

1. Within the framework of their education systems, the Parties shall recognise that persons belonging to a national minority have the right to set up and to manage their own private educational and training establishments.

2. The exercise of this right shall not entail any financial obligation for the Parties.

Article 14

1. The Parties undertake to recognise that every person belonging to a national minority has the right to learn his or her minority language.

2. In areas inhabited by persons belonging to national minorities traditionally or in substantial numbers, if there is sufficient demand, the Parties shall endeavour to ensure, as far as possible and within the framework of their education systems, that persons belonging to those minorities have adequate opportunities for being taught the minority

118

language or for receiving instruction in this language.

3. Paragraph 2 of this artide shall be implemented without prejudice to the learning of the official language or the teaching in this language.

Article 15

The Parties shall create the conditions necessary for the effective participation of persons belonging to national minorities in cultural, social and economic life and in public affairs, in particular those affecting them.

Article 16

The Parties shall refrain from measures which alter the proportions of the population in areas inhabited by persons belonging to national minorities and are aimed at restricting the rights and freedoms flowing from the principles enshrined in the present framework Convention.

Article 17

1. The Parties undertake not to interfere with the right of persons belonging to national minorities to establish and maintain free and peaceful contacts across frontiers with persons lawfully staying in other States, in particular those with whom they share an ethnic, cultural, linguistic or religious identity, or a common cultural heritage.

2. The Parties undertake not to interfere with the right of persons belonging to national minorities to participate in the activities of non-governmental organisations, both at the national and international levels.

Article 18

1. The Parties shall endeavour to conclude, where necessary, bilateral and multilateral agreements with other States, in particular neighbouring States, in order to ensure the protection of persons belonging to the national minorities concerned.

Article 19

The Parties undertake to respect and implement the principles enshrined in the present framework Convention making, where necessary, only those limitations, restrictions or derogations which are provided for in international legal instruments, in particular the Convention for the Protection of Human Rights and Fundamental Freedoms, in so far as they are relevant to the rights and freedoms flowing from the said principles.

Section III

Article 20

In the exercise of the rights and freedoms flowing from the principles enshrined in the present framework Convention, any person belonging to a national minority shall respect the national legislation and the rights of others, in particular those of persons belonging to the majority or to other national minorities.

Article 21

Nothing in the present framework Convention shall be interpreted as implying any right to engage in any activity or perform any act contrary to the fundamental principles of international law and in particular of the sovereign equality, territorial integrity and political independence of States.

Article 22

Nothing in the present framework Convention shall be construed as limiting or derogating from any of the human rights and fundamental freedoms which may be ensured under the laws of any Contracting Party or under any other agreement to which it is a Party.

Article 23

The rights and freedoms flowing from the principles enshrined in the present framework Convention, in so far as they are the subject of a corresponding provision in the Convention for the Protection of Human Rights and Fundamental Freedoms or in the Protocols thereto, shall be understood so as to conform to the latter provisions.

Section IV

Article 24

1. The Committee of Ministers of the Council of Europe shall monitor the implementation of this framework Convention by the Contracting Parties.

2. The Parties which are not members of the Council of Europe shall participate in the implementation mechanism, according to modalities to be determined.

Article 25

1. Within a period of one year following the entry into force of this framework Convention in respect of a Contracting Party, the latter shall transmit to the Secretary General of the Council of Europe full information on the legislative and other measures taken to give effect to the principles set out in this framework Convention.

2. Thereafter, each Party shall transmit to the Secretary General on a periodical basis and whenever the Committee of Ministers so requests any further information of relevance to the implementation of this framework Convention.

3. The Secretary General shall forward to the Committee of Ministers the information transmitted under the terms of this Article.

Article 26

1. In evaluating the adequacy of the measures taken by the Parties to give effect to the principles set out in this framework Convention the Committee of Ministers shall be assisted by an advisory committee, the members of which shall have recognised expertise in the field of the protection of national minorities.

2. The composition of this advisory committee and its procedure shall be determined by the Committee of Ministers within a period of one year following the entry into force of this framework Convention.

Section V

Article 27

This framework Convention shall be open for signature by the member

States of the Council of Europe. Up until the date when the Convention enters into force, it shall also be open for signature by any other State so invited by the Committee of Ministers. It is subject to ratification, acceptance or approval. Instruments of ratification, acceptance or approval shall be deposited with the Secretary General of the Council of Europe.

Article 28

1. This framework Convention shall enter into force on the first day of the month following the expiration of a period of three months after the date on which twelve member States of the Council of Europe have expressed their consent to be bound by the Convention in accordance with the provisions of Article 27.

2. In respect of any member State which subsequently expresses its consent to be bound by it, the framework Convention shall enter into force on the first day of the month following the expiration of a period of three months after the date of the deposit of the instrument of ratification, acceptance or approval.

Article 29

1. After the entry into force of this framework Convention and after consulting the Contracting States, the Committee of Ministers of the Council of Europe may invite to accede to the Convention, by a decision taken by the majority provided for in Article 20.d of the Statute of the Council of Europe, any non-member State of the Council of Europe which, invited to sign in accordance with the provisions of Article 27, has not yet done so, and any other non-member State.

2. In respect of any acceding State, the framework Convention shall enter into force on the first day of the month following the expiration of a period of three months after the date of the deposit of the instrument of accession with the Secretary General of the Council of Europe.

Article 30

1. Any State may, at the time of signature or when depositing its instrument of ratification, acceptance, approval or accession, specify the territory or territories for whose international relations it is responsible to

which this framework Convention shall apply.

2. Any State may at any later date, by a declaration addressed to the Secretary General of the Council of Europe, extend the application of this framework Convention to any other territory specified in the declaration. In respect of such territory the framework Convention shall enter into force on the first day of the month following the expiration of a period of three months after the date of receipt of such declaration by the Secretary General.

3. Any declaration made under the two preceding paragraphs may, in respect of any territory specified in such declaration, be withdrawn by a notification addressed to the Secretary General. The withdrawal shall become effective on the first day of the month following the expiration of a period of three months after the date of receipt of such notification by the Secretary General.

Article 31

1. Any Party may at any time denounce this framework Convention by means of a notification addressed to the Secretary General of the Council of Europe.

2. Such denunciation shall become effective on the first day of the month following the expiration of a period of six months after the date of receipt of the notification by the Secretary General.

Article 32

1. The Secretary General of the Council of Europe shall notify the member States of the Council, other signatory States and any State which has acceded to this framework Convention, of:

a. any signature;

b. the deposit of any instrument of ratification, acceptance, approval or accession;

c. any date of entry into force of this framework Convention in accordance with
Articles 28, 29 and 30;

123

any other act, notification or communication relating to this framework Convention.

In witness whereof the undersigned, being duly authorised thereto, have signed this framework Convention.

Done at .., this ..day of .., in English and French, both texts being equally authentic, in a single copy which shall be deposited in the archives of the Council of Europe. The Secretary General of the Council of Europe shall transmit certified copies to each member State of the Council of Europe and to any State invited to sign or accede to this framework Convention.

[NOTE: Adopted by the Committee of Ministers on 10 November 1994.]

Explanatory report
on the framework Convention
for the protection of national minorities

BACKGROUND

1. The Council of Europe has examined the situation of national minorities on a number of occasions over a period of more than forty years. Already in its very first year of existence (1919), the Parliamentary Assembly recognised, in a report of its Committee on Legal and Administrative Questions, the importance of "the problem of wider protection of the rights of national minorities". In 1961, the Assembly recommended the inclusion of an article in a second additional protocol to guarantee to national minorities certain rights not covered by the European Convention on Human Rights (ECHR). The latter simply refers to "association with a national minority" in the non-discrimination clause provided for in Article 14. Recommendation 285 (1961) proposed the following wording for the draft article on the protection of national minorities:

> "Persons belonging to a national minority shall not be denied the right, in community with the other members of their group, and as far as compatible with public order, to enjoy their own culture, to use their own language, to establish their schools and receive teaching in the language of their choice or to profess and practise their own

2. The Committee of Experts, which had been instructed to consider whether it was possible and advisable to draw up such a protocol, adjourned its activities until a final decision had been reached on the Belgian linguistics cases concerning the language used in education (Eur. Court H.R. Judgment of 27 July 1968, Series A No 6). In 1973 it concluded that, from a legal point of view, there was no special need to make the rights of minorities the subject of a further protocol to the ECHR. However, the experts considered that there was no major legal obstacle to the adoption of such a protocol if it were considered advisable for other reasons.

3. More recently, the Parliamentary Assembly recommended a number of political and legal measures to the Committee of Ministers, in particular the drawing up of a protocol or a convention on the rights of national

minorities. Recommendation 1134 (1990) contains a list of principles which the Assembly considered necessary for the protection of national minorities. In October 1991, the Steering Committee for Human Rights (CDDH) was given the task of considering, from both a legal and a political point of view, the conditions in which the Council of Europe could undertake an activity for the protection of national minorities, taking into account the work done by the Conference on Security and Co-operation in Europe (CSCE) and the United Nations, and the reflections within the Council of Europe.

4. In May 1992, the Committee of Ministers instructed the CDDH to examine the possibility of formulating specific legal standards relating to the protection of national minorities. To this end, the CDDH established a committee of experts (DH-MIN) which, under new terms of reference issued in March 1993, was required to propose specific legal standards in this area, bearing in mind the principle of complementarity of work between the Council of Europe and the CSCE. The CDDH and the DH-MIN took various texts into account, in particular the proposal for a European Convention for the Protection of National Minorities drawn up by the European Commission for democracy through law (the so-called Venice Commission), the Austrian proposal for an additional protocol to the ECHR, the draft additional protocol to the ECHR included in Assembly Recommendation 1201 (1993) and other proposals. This examination culminated in the report of the CDDH to the Committee of Ministers of 8 September 1993, which included various legal standards which might be adopted in this area and the legal instruments in which they could be laid down. In this connection, the CDDH noted that there was no consensus on the interpretation of the term "national minorities".

5. The decisive step was taken when the Heads of State and Government of the Council of Europe's member States met in Vienna at the Summit of 8 and 9 October 1993. There, it was agreed that the national minorities which the upheavals of history have established in Europe had to be protected and respected as a contribution to peace and stability. In particular, the Heads of State and Government decided to enter into legal commitments regarding the protection of national minorities. Appendix II of the Vienna Declaration instructed the Committee of Ministers:

- to draft with minimum delay a framework convention specifying the principles which contracting States commit themselves to

126

respect, in order to assure the protection of national minorities. This instrument would also be open for signature by non-member States.

- to begin work on drafting a protocol complementing the European Convention on Human Rights in the cultural field by provisions guaranteeing individual rights, in particular for persons belonging to national minorities.

6. On 4 November 1993, the Committee of Ministers established an ad hoc Committee for the Protection of National Minorities (CAHMIN). Its terms of reference reflected the decisions taken in Vienna. The Committee, made up of experts from the Council of Europe's member States, started work in late January 1994, with the participation of representatives of the CDDH, the Council for Cultural Co-operation (CDCC), the Steering Committee on the Mass Media (CDMM) and the European Commission for democracy through law. The High Commissioner on National Minorities of the CSCE and the Commission of the European Communities also took part, as observers.

7.   On 15 April 1994, CAHMIN submitted an interim report to the Committee of Ministers, which was then communicated to the Parliamentary Assembly (Doc. 7109). At its 94th session in May 1994, the Committee of Ministers expressed satisfaction with the progress achieved under the terms of reference flowing from the Vienna Declaration.

8. A certain number of provisions of the framework Convention requiring political arbitration as well as those concerning the monitoring of the implementation were drafted by the Committee of Ministers (517bis meeting of Ministers' Deputies, 7 October 1994).

9.   At its meeting from 10 to 14 October 1994, CAHMIN decided to submit the draft framework Convention to the Committee of Ministers, which adopted the text at the 95th Ministerial Session on 10 November 1994. The framework Convention was opened for signature by the Council of Europe's member States on February 1, 1995

GENERAL CONSIDERATIONS
Objectives of the framework Convention

10. The framework Convention is the first legally binding multilateral

instrument devoted to the protection of national minorities in general. Its aim is to specify the legal principles which States undertake to respect in order to ensure the protection of national minorities. The Council of Europe has thereby given effect to the Vienna Declaration's call (Appendix II) for the political commitments adopted by the Conference on Security and Co-operation in Europe (CSCE) to be transformed, to the greatest possible extent, into legal obligations.

Approaches and fundamental concepts

11. In view of the range of different situations and problems to be resolved, a choice was made for a framework Convention which contains mostly programme-type provisions setting out objectives which the Parties undertake to pursue. These provisions, which will not be directly applicable, leave the States concerned a measure of discretion in the implementation of the objectives which they have undertaken to achieve, thus enabling them to take particular circumstances into account.

12. It should also be pointed out that the framework Convention contains no definition of the notion of "national minority". It was decided to adopt a pragmatic approach, based on the recognition that at this stage, it is impossible to arrive at a definition capable of mustering general support of all Council of Europe member States.

13. The implementation of the principles set out in this framework Convention shall be done through national legislation and appropriate governmental policies. It does not imply the recognition of collective rights. The emphasis is placed on the protection of persons belonging to national minorities, who may exercise their rights individually and in community with others (see Article 3, paragraph 2). In this respect, the framework Convention follows the approach of texts adopted by other international organisations.

Structure of the framework Convention

14. Apart from its preamble, the framework Convention contains an operative part which is divided into five sections.

15. Section I contains provisions which, in a general fashion, stipulate certain fundamental principles which may serve to elucidate the other

substantive provisions of the framework Convention.

16. Section II contains a catalogue of specific principles.

17. Section III contains various provisions concerning the interpretation and application of the framework Convention.

18. Section IV contains provisions on the monitoring of the implementation of the framework Convention.

19. Section V contains the final clauses which are based on the model final clauses for conventions and agreements concluded within the Council of Europe.

COMMENTARY ON THE PROVISIONS OF THE FRAMEWORK CONVENTION

PREAMBLE

20. The preamble sets out the reasons for drawing up this framework Convention and explains certain basic concerns of its drafters. The opening words already indicate that this instrument may be signed and ratified by States not members of the Council of Europe (see Article 27).

21. The preamble refers to the statutory aim of the Council of Europe and to one of the methods by which this aim is to be pursued: the maintenance and further realisation of human rights and fundamental freedoms.

22. Reference is also made to the Vienna Declaration of Heads of State and Government of the member States of the Council of Europe, a document which laid the foundation for the present framework Convention (see also paragraph 5 above). In fact, the text of the preamble is largely inspired by that Declaration, in particular its Appendix II. The same is true of the choice of undertakings included in Sections I and II of the framework Convention.

23. The preamble mentions, in a non-exhaustive way, three further sources of inspiration for the content of the framework Convention: the European Convention for the Protection of Human Rights and Fundamental Freedoms (ECHR) and instruments which contain commitments regarding the protection of national minorities of the United Nations and the CSCE.

24. The preamble reflects the concern of the Council of Europe and its member States about the jeopardy to the existence of national minorities and is inspired by Article 1, paragraph 1 of the United Nations Declaration on the Rights of Persons belonging to National or Ethnic, Religious and Linguistic Minorities (Resolution 47/135 adopted by the General Assembly on 18 December 1992).

25. Given that the framework Convention is also open to States which are not members of the Council of Europe, and to ensure a more comprehensive approach, it was decided to include certain principles from which flow rights and freedoms which are already guaranteed in the ECHR or in the protocols thereto (see also in connection with this, Article 23 of the framework Convention).

26. The reference to United Nations Conventions and declarations recalls the work done at the universal level, for example in the Covenant on Civil and Political Rights (Article 27) and in the Declaration on the Rights of Persons belonging to National Ethnic, Religious and Linguistic Minorities. However this reference does not extend to any definition of a national minority which may be contained in these texts.

27. The reference to the relevant CSCE commitments reflects the desire expressed in Appendix II of the Vienna Declaration that the Council of Europe should apply itself to transforming, to the greatest possible extent, these political commitments into legal obligations. The Copenhagen Document in particular provided guidance for drafting the framework Convention.

28. The penultimate paragraph in the preamble sets out the main aim of the framework Convention: to ensure the effective protection of national minorities and of the rights of persons belonging to those minorities. It also stresses that the effective protection should be ensured within the rule of law, respecting the territorial integrity and national sovereignty of states.

29. The purpose of the last recital is to indicate that the provisions of this framework Convention are not directly applicable. It is not concerned with the law and practice of the Parties in regard to the reception of international treaties in the internal legal order.

SECTION I

Article 1

30. The main purpose of Article 1 is to specify that the protection of national minorities, which forms an integral part of the protection of human rights, does not fall within the reserved domain of states. The statement that this protection "forms an integral part of the international protection of human rights" does not confer any competence to interpret the present framework Convention on the organs established by the ECHR.

31. The article refers to the protection of national minorities as such and of the rights and freedoms of persons belonging to such minorities. This distinction and the difference in wording make it clear that no collective rights of national minorities are envisaged (see also the commentary to Article 3). The Parties do however recognise that protection of a national minority can be achieved through protection of the rights of individuals belonging to such a minority.

Article 2

32. This article provides a set of principles governing the application of the framework Convention. It is, inter alia, inspired by the United Nations Declaration on Principles of International Law concerning Friendly Relations and Co-operation among States in accordance with the Charter of the United Nations (General Assembly Resolution 2625 (XXV) of 24 October 1970). The principles mentioned in this provision are of a general nature but do have particular relevance to the field covered by the framework Convention.

Article 3

33. This article contains two distinct but related principles laid down in two different paragraphs.

Paragraph 1

34. Paragraph 1 firstly guarantees to every person belonging to a national minority the freedom to choose to be treated or not to be treated as such. This provision leaves it to every such person to decide whether or not he or

she wishes to come under the protection flowing from the principles of the framework Convention.

35. This paragraph does not imply a right for an individual to choose arbitrarily to belong to any national minority. The individual's subjective choice is inseparably linked to objective criteria relevant to the person's identity.

36. Paragraph 1 further provides that no disadvantage shall arise from the free choice it guarantees, or from the exercise of the rights which are connected to that choice. This part of the provision aims to secure that the enjoyment of the freedom to choose shall also not be impaired indirectly.

Paragraph 2

37. Paragraph 2 provides that the rights and freedoms flowing from the principles of the framework Convention may be exercised individually or in community with others. It thus recognises the possibility of joint exercise of those rights and freedoms, which is distinct from the notion of collective rights . The term "others" shall be understood in the widest possible sense and shall include persons belonging to the same national minority, to another national minority, or to the majority.

SECTION II

Article 4

38. The purpose of this article is to ensure the applicability of the principles of equality and non-discrimination for persons belonging to national minorities. The provisions of this Article are to be understood in the context of this framework Convention.

Paragraphs 1 and 2

39. Paragraph 1 takes the classic approach to these principles. Paragraph 2 stresses that the promotion of full and effective equality between persons belonging to a national minority and those belonging to the majority may require the Parties to adopt special measures that take into account the specific conditions of the persons concerned. Such measures need to be "adequate", i.e. in conformity with the proportionality principle, in order to

132

avoid violation of the rights of others as well as discrimination against others. This principle requires, among other things, that such measures do not extend, in time or in scope, beyond what is necessary in order to achieve the aim of full and effective equality.

40. No separate provision dealing specifically with the principle of equal opportunities has been included in the framework Convention. Such an inclusion was considered unnecessary as the principle is already implied in paragraph 2 of this article. Given the principle of non-discrimination set out in paragraph 1 the same was considered true for freedom of movement.

Paragraph 3

41. The purpose of paragraph 3 is to make clear that the measures referred to in paragraph 2 are not to be regarded as contravening the principles of equality and non-discrimination. Its aim is to ensure to persons belonging to national minorities effective equality along with persons belonging to the majority.

Article 5

42. This Article essentially aims at ensuring that persons belonging to national minorities can maintain and develop their culture and preserve their identity.

Paragraph 1

43. Paragraph 1 contains an obligation to promote the necessary conditions in this respect. It lists four essential elements of the identity of a national minority. This provision does not imply that all ethnic, cultural, linguistic or religious differences necessarily lead to the creation of national minorities (see in this regard the report of the CSCE meeting of experts, held in Geneva in 1991, section II paragraph 4).

44. The reference to "traditions" is not an endorsement or acceptance of practices which are contrary to national law or international standards. Traditional practices remain subject to limitations arising from the requirements of public order.

Paragraph 2

45. The purpose of paragraph 2 is to protect persons belonging to national minorities from assimilation against their will. It does not prohibit voluntary assimilation.

46. Paragraph 2 does not preclude the Parties from taking measures in pursuance of their general integration policy. It thus acknowledges the importance of social cohesion and reflects the desire expressed in the preamble that cultural diversity be a source and a factor, not of division, but of enrichment to each society.

Article 6

47. This article is an expression of the concerns stated in Appendix III to the Vienna Declaration (Declaration and Plan of Action on combating racism, xenophobia, antisemitism and intolerance).

Paragraph 1

48. Paragraph 1 stresses a spirit of tolerance and intercultural dialogue and points out the importance of the Parties' promoting mutual respect, understanding and co-operation among all who live on their territory. The fields of education, culture and the media are specifically mentioned because they are considered particularly relevant to the achievement of these aims.

49. In order to strengthen social cohesion, the aim of this paragraph is, inter alia, to promote tolerance and intercultural dialogue, by eliminating barriers between persons belonging to ethnic, cultural, linguistic and religious groups through the encouragement of intercultural organisations and movements which seek to promote mutual respect and understanding and to integrate these persons into society whilst preserving their identity.

Paragraph 2

50. This provision is inspired by paragraph 40.2 of the Copenhagen Document of the CSCE. This obligation aims at the protection of all persons who may be subject to threats or acts of discrimination, hostility or violence, irrespective of the source of such threats or acts.

Article 7

51. The purpose of this article is to guarantee respect for the right of every person belonging to a national minority to the fundamental freedoms mentioned therein. These freedoms are of course of a universal nature, i.e. they apply to all persons, whether belonging to a national minority or not (see, for instance, the corresponding provisions in Articles 9, 10 and 11 of the ECHR), but they are particularly relevant for the protection of national minorities. For the reasons stated above in the commentary on the preamble, it was decided to include certain undertakings which already appear in the ECHR.

52. This provision may imply for the Parties certain positive obligations to protect the freedoms mentioned against violations which do not emanate from the State. Under the ECHR, the possibility of such positive obligations has been recognised by the European Court of Human Rights.

53. Some of the freedoms laid down in Article 7 are elaborated upon in Articles 8 and 9.

Article 8

54. This article lays down more detailed rules for the protection of freedom of religion than Article 7. It combines several elements from paragraphs 32.2, 32.3 and 32.6 of the CSCE Copenhagen Document into a single provision. This freedom of course applies to all persons and persons belonging to a national minority should, in accordance with Article 4, enjoy it as well. Given the importance of this freedom in the present context, it was felt particularly appropriate to give it special attention.

Article 9

55. This article contains more detailed rules for the protection of the freedom of expression than Article 7.

Paragraph 1

56. The first sentence of this paragraph is modelled on the second sentence of Article 10, paragraph 1, ECHR. Although the sentence refers specifically to the freedom to receive and impart information and ideas in the minority

language, it also implies the freedom to receive and impart information and ideas in the majority or other languages.

57. The second sentence of this paragraph contains an undertaking to ensure that there is no discrimination in access to the media. The words "in the framework of their legal systems" were inserted in order to respect constitutional provisions which may limit the extent to which a Party can regulate access to the media.

Paragraph 2

58. This paragraph is modelled on the third sentence of Article 10, paragraph 1, ECHR.

59. The licensing of sound radio and television broadcasting, and of cinema enterprises should be non-discriminatory and be based on objective criteria. The inclusion of these requirements, which are not expressly mentioned in the third sentence of Article 10, paragraph 1, ECHR, was considered important for an instrument designed to protect persons belonging to a national minority.

60. The words "sound radio", which also appear in paragraph 3 of this Article, do not appear in the corresponding sentence in Article 10 ECHR. They are used in order to reflect modern terminology and do not imply any material difference in meaning from Article 10 ECHR.

Paragraph 3

61. The first sentence of this paragraph, dealing with the creation and use of printed media, contains an essentially negative undertaking whereas the more flexibly worded second sentence emphasises a positive obligation in the field of sound radio and television broadcasting (e.g. the allocation of frequencies). This distinction reflects the relative scarcity of available frequencies and the need for regulation in the latter field. No express reference has been made to the right of persons belonging to a national minority to seek funds for the establishment of media, as this right was considered self-evident.

Paragraph 4

62. This paragraph emphasises the need for special measures with the dual aim of facilitating access to the media for persons belonging to national minorities and promoting tolerance and cultural pluralism. The expression "adequate measures" was used for the reasons given in the commentary on Article 4, paragraph 2 (see paragraph 39), which uses the same words. The paragraph complements the undertaking laid down in the last sentence of Article 9, paragraph 1. The measures envisaged by this paragraph could, for example, consist of funding for minority broadcasting or for programme productions dealing with minority issues and/or offering a dialogue between groups, or of encouraging, subject to editorial independence, editors and broadcasters to allow national minorities access to their media.

Article 10

Paragraph 1

63. The recognition of the right of every person belonging to a national minority to use his or her minority language freely and without interference is particularly important. The use of the minority language represents one of the principal means by which such persons can assert and preserve their identity. It also enables them to exercise their freedom of expression. "In public" means, for instance, in a public place, outside, or in the presence of other persons but is not concerned in any circumstances with relations with public authorities, the subject of paragraph 2 of this article.

Paragraph 2

64. This provision does not cover all relations between individuals belonging to national minorities and public authorities. It only extends to administrative authorities. Nevertheless, the latter must be broadly interpreted to include, for example, ombudsmen. In recognition of the possible financial, administrative, in particular in the military field, and technical difficulties associated with the use of minority languages in relations between persons belonging to national minorities and the administrative authorities, this provision has been worded very flexibly, leaving Parties a wide measure of discretion.

65. Once the two conditions in paragraph 2 are met, Parties shall endeavour to ensure the use of a minority language in relations with the administrative authorities as far as possible. The existence of a "real need" is to be assessed

by the State on the basis of objective criteria. Although contracting States should make every effort to apply this principle, the wording "as far as possible" indicates that various factors, in particular the financial resources of the Party concerned, may be taken into consideration.

66. The Parties' obligations regarding the use of minority languages do not in any way affect the status of the official language or languages of the country concerned. Moreover, the framework Convention deliberately refrains from defining "areas inhabited by persons belonging to national minorities traditionally or in substantial numbers". It was considered preferable to adopt a flexible form of wording which will allow each Party's particular circumstances to be taken into account. The term "inhabited ... traditionally" does not refer to historical minorities, but only to those still living in the same geographical area (see also Article 11 paragraph 3 and Article 14 paragraph 2)

Paragraph 3

67. This paragraph is based on certain provisions contained in articles 5 and 6 of the European Convention on Human Rights. It does not go beyond the safeguards contained in those articles.

Article 11

Paragraph 1

68. In view of the practical implications of this obligation, the provision is worded in such a way as to enable Parties to apply it in the light of their own particular circumstances. For example, Parties may use the alphabet of their official language to write the name(s) of a person belonging to a national minority in its phonetic form. Persons who have been forced to give up their original name(s), or whose name(s) has (have) been changed by force, should be entitled to revert to it (them), subject of course to exceptions in the case of abuse of rights and changes of name(s) for fraudulent purposes. It is understood that the legal systems of the Parties will, in this respect, meet international principles concerning the protection of national minorities.

Paragraph 2

69. The obligation in this paragraph concerns an individual's right to display "in his or her minority language signs, inscriptions and other information of a private nature visible to the public". This does not, of course, exclude persons belonging to national minorities from being required to use, in addition, the official language and/or other minority languages. The expression "of a private nature" refers to all that is not official.

Paragraph 3

70. This article aims to promote the possibility of having local names, street names and other topographical indications intended for the public also in the minority language. In implementing this principle the States are entitled to take due account of the specific circumstances and the framework of their legal systems, including, where appropriate, agreements with other States. In the field covered by this provision, it is understood that the Parties are under no obligation to conclude agreements with other States. Conversely, the possibility of concluding such agreements is not ruled out. It is also understood that the legally binding nature of existing agreements remains unaffected. This provision does not imply any official recognition of local names in the minority languages.

Article 12

71. This article seeks to promote knowledge of the culture, history, language and religion of both national minorities and the majority population in an intercultural perspective (see Article 6, paragraph 1). The aim is to create a climate of tolerance and dialogue, as referred to in the preamble to the framework Convention and in Appendix II of the Vienna Declaration of the Heads of State and Government. The list in the second paragraph is not exhaustive whilst the words "access to textbooks" are understood as including the publication of textbooks and their purchase in other countries. The obligation to promote equal opportunities for access to education at all levels for persons belonging to national minorities reflects a concern expressed in the Vienna Declaration.

Article 13
Paragraph 1

72. The Parties' obligation to recognise the right of persons belonging to national minorities to set up and manage their own private educational and

training establishments is subject to the requirements of their educational system, particularly the regulations relating to compulsory schooling. The establishments covered by this paragraph may be subject to the same forms of supervision as other establishments, particularly with regard to teaching standards. Once the required standards are met, it is important that any qualifications awarded are officially recognised. The relevant national legislation must be based on objective criteria and conform to the principle of non-discrimination.

Paragraph 2

73. The exercise of the right referred to in paragraph 1 does not entail any financial obligation for the Party concerned, but neither does it exclude the possibility of such a contribution.

Article 14

Paragraph 1

74. The obligation to recognise the right of every person belonging to a national minority to learn his or her minority language concerns one of the principal means by which such individuals can assert and preserve their identity. There can be no exceptions to this. Without prejudice to the principles mentioned in paragraph 2, this paragraph does not imply positive action, notably of a financial nature, on the part of the State.

Paragraph 2

75. This provision concerns teaching of and instruction in a minority language. In recognition of the possible financial, administrative and technical difficulties associated with instruction of or in minority languages, this provision has been worded very flexibly, leaving Parties a wide measure of discretion. The obligation to endeavour to ensure instruction of or in minority languages is subject to several conditions; in particular, there must be "sufficient demand" from persons belonging to the relevant national minorities. The wording "as far as possible" indicates that such instruction is dependent on the available resources of the Party concerned.

76. The text deliberately refrains from defining "sufficient demand", a flexible form of wording which allows Parties to take account of their

countries' own particular circumstances. Parties have a choice of means and arrangements in ensuring such instruction, taking their particular educational system into account.

77. The alternatives referred to in this paragraph - "... opportunities for being taught the minority language or for receiving instruction in this language" - are not mutually exclusive. Even though Article 14 paragraph 2 imposes no obligation upon States to do both, its wording does not prevent the States Parties from implementing the teaching of the minority language as well as the instruction in the minority language. Bilingual instruction may be one of the means of achieving the objective of this provision. The obligation arising from this paragraph could be extended to pre-school education.

Paragraph 3

78. The opportunities for being taught the minority language or for receiving instruction in this language are without prejudice to the learning of the official language or the teaching in this language. Indeed, knowledge of the official language is a factor of social cohesion and integration.

79. It is for States where there is more than one official language to settle the particular questions which the implementation of this provision shall entail.

Article 15

80. This article requires Parties to create the conditions necessary for the effective participation of persons belonging to national minorities in cultural, social and economic life and in public affairs, in particular those affecting them. It aims above all to encourage real equality between persons belonging to national minorities and those forming part of the majority. In order to create the necessary conditions for such participation by persons belonging to national minorities, Parties could promote - in the framework of their constitutional systems - inter alia the following measures:

- consultation with these persons, by means of appropriate procedures and, in particular, through their representative institutions, when Parties are contemplating legislation or administrative measures likely to affect them directly;

- involving these persons in the preparation, implementation and assessment of national and regional development plans and programmes likely to affect them directly;

- undertaking studies, in conjunction with these persons, to assess the possible impact on them of projected development activities.

- effective participation of persons belonging to national minorities in the decision making processes and elected bodies both at national and local levels;

- decentralised or local forms of government.

Article 16

81. The purpose of this article is to protect against measures which change the proportion of the population in areas inhabited by persons belonging to national minonties and are aimed at restricting the rights and freedoms which flow from the present framework Convention. Examples of such measures might be expropriation, evictions and expulsions or redrawing administrative borders with a view to restricting the enjoyment of such rights and freedoms ("gerrymandering").

82. The article prohibits only measures which are aimed at restricting the rights and freedoms flowing from the framework Convention. It was considered impossible to extend the prohibition to measures having the effect of restricting such rights and freedoms, since such measures may sometimes be entirely justified and legitimate. One example might be resettlement of inhabitants of a village in order to build a dam.

Article 17

83. This article contains two undertakings important to the maintenance and development of the culture of persons belonging to a national minority and to the preservation of their identity (see also Article 5, paragraph 1). The first paragraph deals with the right to establish and maintain free and peaceful contacts across frontiers, whereas the second paragraph protects the right to participate in the activities of non-governmental organisations (see also in this connection, the provisions on freedom of assembly and of

association in Article 7).

84. The provisions of this article are largely based on paragraphs 32.4 and 32.6 of the Copenhagen Document of the CSCE. It was considered unnecessary to include an explicit provision on the right to establish and maintain contacts within the territory of a State, since this was felt to be adequately covered by other provisions of the framework Convention, notably Article 7 as regards freedom of assembly and of association.

Article 18

85. This article encourages the Parties to conclude, in addition to the existing international instruments, and where the specific circumstances justify it, bilateral and multilateral agreements for the protection of national minorities. It also stimulates transfrontier co-operation. As is emphasised in the Vienna Declaration and its Appendix II, such agreements and co-operation are important for the promotion of tolerance, prosperity, stability and peace.

Paragraph 1

86. Bilateral and multilateral agreements as envisaged by this paragraph might, for instance, be concluded in the fields of culture, education and information.

Paragraph 2

87. This paragraph points out the importance of transfrontier co-operation. Exchange of information and experience between States is an important tool for the promotion of mutual understanding and confidence. In particular, transfrontier co-operation has the advantage that it allows for arrangements specifically tailored to the wishes and needs of the persons concerned.

Article 19

88. This article provides for the possibility of limitations, restrictions or derogations. When the undertakings included in this framework Convention have an equivalent in other international legal instruments, in particular the ECHR, only the limitations, restrictions or derogations provided for in those instruments are allowed. When the undertakings set forth in this

framework Convention have no equivalent in other international legal instruments, the only limitations, restrictions or derogations allowed are those which, included in other legal instruments (such as the ECHR) in respect of different undertakings, are relevant.

SECTION III

Article 20

89. Persons belonging to national minorities are required to respect the national Constitution and other national legislation. However, this reference to national legislation clearly does not entitle Parties to ignore the provisions of the framework Convention. Persons belonging to national minorities must also respect the rights of others. In this regard, reference may be made to situations where persons belonging to national minorities are in a minority nationally but form a majority within one area of the State.

Article 21

90. This provision stresses the importance of the fundamental principles of international law and specifies that the protection of persons belonging to national minorities must be in accordance with these principles.

Article 22

91. This provision, which is based on Article 60 of the ECHR, sets out a well-known principle. The aim is to ensure that persons belonging to national minorities benefit from whichever of the relevant national or international human rights legislation is most favourable to them.

Article 23

92. This provision deals with the relationship between the framework Convention and the European Convention on Human Rights, reference to which is included in the preamble. Under no circumstances can the framework Convention modify the rights and freedoms safeguarded in the European Convention on Human Rights. On the contrary, rights and freedoms enshrined in the framework Convention which are the subject of a corresponding provision in the European Convention on Human Rights

144

must be interpreted in accordance with the latter.

SECTION IV

Articles 24-26

93. To provide for overseeing the application of the framework Convention, the Committee of Ministers is entrusted with the task of monitoring the implementation by the Contracting Parties. The Committee of Ministers shall determine the modalities for the participation in the implementation mechanism by the Parties which are not members of the Council of Europe.

94. Each Party shall transmit to the Secretary General on a periodical basis and whenever the Committee of Ministers so requests information of relevance to the implementation of this framework Convention. The Secretary General shall transmit this information to the Committee of Ministers. However, the first report, the aim of which is to provide full information on legislative and other measures which the Party has taken to give effect to the undertakings set out in the framework Convention, must be submitted within one year of the entry into force of the framework Convention in respect of the party concerned. The purpose of the subsequent reports shall be to complement the information included in the first report.

95. In order to ensure the efficiency of the monitoring of the implementation of the Convention, it provides for the setting up of an advisory committee. The task of this advisory committee is to assist the Committee of Ministers when it evaluates the adequacy of the measures taken by a Party to give effect to the principles set out in the framework Convention.

96. It is up to the Committee of Ministers to determine, within one year of the entry into force of the framework Convention, the composition and the procedures of the advisory committee, the members of which shall have recognised expertise in the field of the protection of national minorities.

97. The monitoring of the implementation of this framework Convention shall, in so far as possible, be transparent. In this regard it would be advisable to envisage the publication of the reports and other texts resulting from such monitoring.

SECTION V

98. The final provisions, contained in articles 27 to 32 are based on the model final clauses for conventions and agreements concluded within the Council of Europe. No article on reservations was included; reservations are allowed in as far as they are permitted by international law. Apart from Articles 27 and 29 the articles in this section require no particular comment.

Articles 27 and 29

99. The framework Convention is open for signature by the Council of Europe's member States and, at the invitation of the Committee of Ministers, by other States. It is understood that "other States" are those States which participate in the Conference on Security and Co-operation in Europe. These provisions take account of the Vienna Declaration, according to which the framework Convention should also be open for signature by non-member States (see Appendix II to the Vienna Declaration of the Council of Europe Summit).

COUNCIL OF EUROPE
CONSEIL DE L'EUROPE

EUROPEAN CHARTER
OF LOCAL SELF-GOVERNMENT

CHARTE EUROPEENNE
DE L'AUTONOMIE LOCALE

STRASBOURG, 15. X. 1985

P R E A M B L E

The member States of the Council of Europe, signatory hereto,

Considering that the aim of the Council of Europe is to achieve a greater unity between its members for the purpose of safeguarding and realising the ideals and principles which are their common heritage;

Considering that one of the methods by which this aim is to be achieved is through agreements in the administrative field;

Considering that the local authorities are one of the main foundations of any democratic regime:

Considering that the right of citizens to participate in the conduct of public affairs is one of the democratic principles that are shared by all member States of the Council of Europe;

Convinced that it is at local level that this right can be most directly exercised;

Convinced that the existence of local authorities with real responsibilities can provide an administration which is both effective and close to the citizen;

Aware that the safeguarding and reinforcement of local self-government in the different European countries is an important contribution to the construction of a Europe based on the principles of democracy and the decentralisation of power;

Asserting that this entails the existence of local authorities endowed with democratically constituted decision-making bodies and possessing a wide degree of autonomy with regard to their responsibilities, the ways and means by which those responsibilities are exercised and the resources required for their fulfilment;

Have agreed as follows:

Article I

The Parties undertake to consider themselves bound by the following articles in the manner and to the extent prescribed in Article 12 of this Charter.

PART I

Article 2

Constitutional and legal foundation for local self-government

The principle of local self-government shall be recognised in domestic legislation, and where practicable in the constitution.

Article 3

Concept of local self-government

1. Local self-government denotes the right and the ability of local authorities, within the limits of the law, to regulate and manage a substantial share of public affairs under their own responsibility and in the interests of the local population.

2. This right shall be exercised by councils or assemblies composed of

members freely elected by secret ballot on the basis of direct, equal, universal suffrage, and which may possess executive organs responsible to them. This provision shall in no way affect recourse to assemblies of citizens, referendums or any other form of direct citizen participation where it is permitted by statute.

Article 4

Scope of local self-government

1. The basic powers and responsibilities of local authorities shall be prescribed by the constitution or by statute. However, this provision shall not prevent the attribution to local authorities of powers and responsibilities for specific purposes in accordance with the law.
2. Local authorities shall within the limits of the law have full discretion to exercise their initiative with regard to any matter which is not excluded from their competence nor assigned to any other authority.

3. Public responsibilities shall generally be exercised, in preference, by those authorities which are closest to the citizen. Allocation of responsibility to another authority should weigh up the extent and nature of the task and requirements of efficiency and economy.

4. Powers given to local authorities shall normally be full and exclusive. They may not be undermined or limited by another, central or regional authority except as provided for by the law.

5. Where powers are delegated to them by central or regional authority, local authorities shall, insofar as possible, be allowed discretion in adapting their exercise to local conditions.

6. Local authorities shall be consulted, insofar as possible, in due time and in an appropriate way in the planning and decision-making processes for all matters which concern them directly.

Article 5

Protection of local authority boundaries

Changes in local authority boundaries shall not be made without prior consultation of the local communities concerned, possibly by means of a referendum where this is permitted by statute.

Article 6

Appropriate administrative structures and resources for the tasks of local authorities

1. Without prejudice to more general statutory provisions, local authorities shall be able to determine their own internal administrative structures in order to adapt them to local needs and ensure effective management.

2. The conditions of service of local government employees shall be such as to permit the recruitment of high-quality staff on the basis of merit and competence; to this end adequate training opportunities, remuneration and career prospects shall be provided.

Article 7

Conditions under which responsibilities at local level are exercised

1. The conditions of office of local elected representatives shall provide for free exercise of their functions.

2. They shall allow for appropriate financial compensation for expenses incurred in the exercise of the office in question as well as where appropriate, compensation for loss of earnings or remuneration for work done and corresponding social welfare protection.

3. Any functions and activities which are deemed incompatible with the holding of local elective office shall be determined by statute or fundamental legal principles.

Article 8

Administrative supervision of local authorities' activities
1. Any administrative supervision of local authorities may only be exercised according to such procedures and in such cases as are provided for by the constitution or by statute.

2. Any administrative supervision of the activities of the local authorities shall normally aim only at ensuring compliance with the law and with constitutional principles. Administrative supervision may, however be exercised with regard to expediency by higher local authorities in respect of tasks the execution of which is delegated to local authorities.

3. Administrative supervision of local authorities shall be exercised in such a way as to ensure that the intervention of the controlling authority is kept in proportion to the importance of the interests which it is intended to protect.

Article 9

Financial resources ot local authorities

1. Local authorities shall be entitled, within national economic policy, to adequate financial resources of their own, of which they may dispose freely within the framevork of their powers.

2. Local authorities' financial resources shall be commensurate with the responsibilites provided for by the constitution and the law.

3. Part at least of the financial resources of local authorities shall derive from local taxes and charges of which, within the limits of statute, they have the power to determine the rate.

4. The financial systems on which resources available to local authorities are based shall be of a sufficiently diversified and buoyant nature to enable them to keep pace as far as practically possible with the real evolution of the cost of carrying out their tasks.

5. The protection of financially weaker local authorities calls for the institution of financial equalisation procedures or equivalent measures which are designed to correct the effects of the unequal distribution of potential sources of finance and of the financial burden they must support. Such procedures or measures shall not diminish the discretion local authorities may exercise within their own sphere of responsibility.

6. Local authorities shall be consulted, in an appropriate manner, on the way in which redistributed resources are to be allocated to them.

7. As far as possible, grants to local authorities shall not be earmarked for

the financing of specific projects. The provision of grants shall not remove the basic freedom of local authorities to exercise policy discretion within their own jurisdiction.

8. For the purpose of borrowing for capital investment, local authorities shall have access to the national capital market within the limits of the law.

Article 10

Local authorities' right to associate

1. Local authorities shall be entitled, in exercising their powers, to co-operate and, within the framework of the law, to form consortia with other local authorities in order to carry out tasks of common interest.

2. The entitlement of local authorities to belong to an association for the protection and promotion of their common interests and to belong to an international association of local authorities shall be recognised in each State.

Local authorities shall be entitled, under such conditions as may be provided for by the law, to co-operate with their counterparts in other States.

Article 11

Legal protection of local self-government

Local authorities shall have the right of recourse to a judicial remedy in order to secure free exercise of their powers and respect for such principles of local self-government as are enshrined in the constitution or domestic legislation.

PART II

Miscellaneous provision

Article 12

Undertakings

1. Each Party undertakes to consider itself bound by at least twenty

152

paragraphs of Part I of the Charter, at least ten of which shall be selected from among the following paragraphs:

-Article 2.
-Article 3. paragraphs 1 and 2.
-Article 4. paragraphs 1, 2 and 4.
-Article 5.
-Article 7. paragraph 1.
-Article 8. paragraph 2.
-Article 9. paragraphs 1, 2 and 3.
-Article 10. paragraph 1.
-Article 11.

2. Each Contracting State, when depositing its instrument of ratification, acceptance or approval, shall notify the Secretary General of the Council of Europe of the paragraphs selected in accordance with the provisions of paragraph 1 of this Article.

Any Party may at any later time, notify to the Secretary General that it considers itself bound by any paragraphs of this Charter which it has not already accepted under the terms of paragraph 1 of this Article. Such undertakings subsequently given shall be deemed to be an integral part of the ratification, acceptance or approval of the Party so notifying, and shall have the same effect as from the first day of the month following the expiration of a period of three months after the date of the receipt of the notification by the Secretay General.

Article 13

Authorities to which the Charter applies

The principles of local self-government contained in the present Charter apply to all the categories of local authorities existing within the territory of the Party. However, each Party may, when depositing its instrument of ratification, acceptance or approval, specify the categories of local or regional authorities to which it intends to confine the scope of the Charter or which it intends to exclude from its scope. It may also include further categories of local or regional authorities within the scope of the Charter by subsequent notification to the Secretary General of the Council of Europe.

Article 14

Provision of information

Each Party shall forward to the Secretary General of the Council of Europe all relevant information concerning legislative provisions and other measures taken by it for the purposes of complying with the terms of this Charter.

Part III

Article 15

Signature, ratification and entry into force

1. This Charter shall be open for signature by the member States of the Council of Europe. It is subject to ratification, acceptance or approval. Instruments of ratification, acceptance or approval shall be deposited with the Secretary General of the Council of Europe.

2. This Charter shall enter into force on the first day of the month following the expiration of a period of three months after the date on which four member States of the Council of Europe have expressed their consent to be bound by the Charter in accordance with the provisions of the preceding paragraph.

3. In respect of any member State which subsequently expresses its consent to be bound by it the Charter shall enter into force on the first day of the month following the expiration of a period of three months after the date of the deposit of the instrument of ratification, acceptance or approval.

Article 16

Territorial clause

1. Any State may, at the time of signature or when depositing its instrument of ratification acceptance, approval or accession, specify the territory or territories to which this Charter shall apply.

2 Any State may at any later date, by a declaration addressed to the Secretary

General of he Council of Europe, extend the application of this Charter to any other territory specified in the declaration. In respect of such territory the Charter shall enter into force on the first day of the month following the expiration of a period of three months after the date of receipt of such declaration by the Secretary General.

3. Any declarafion made under the two preceding paragraphs may in respect of any territory specified in such declaration, be withdrawn by a notification addressed to the Secretary General. The withdrawal shall become effective on the first day of the month following the expiration of a period of six months after the date of receipt of such notification by the Secretary General.

Article 17

Denunciation

1. Any Party may denounce this Charter at any time after the expiration of a period of five years from the date on which the Charter entered into force for it. Six month's notice shall be given to the Secretary General of the Council of Europe. Such denunciation shall not affect the validity of the Charter in respect of the other Parties provided that at all times there are not less than four such Parties.

2. Any Party may, in accordance with the provisions set out in the preceding paragraph, denounce any paragraph of Part I of the Charter accepted by it provided that the Party remains bound by the number and type of paragraphs stipulated in Article 12, paragraph 1. Any Party which, upon denouncing a paragraph, no longer meets the requirements of Article 12, paragraph 1 shall be considered as also having denounced the Charter itself.

Article 18

Notifications

The Secretary General of the Council of Europe shall notify the member States of the Council of Europe of:

a. any signature;
b. the deposit of any instrument of ratification, acceptance or approval;
c. any date of entry into force of this Charter in accordance with Article 15;

d. any notification received in application of the provisions of Article 12, paragraphs 2 and 3;

e. any notification received in application of the provisions of Article 13;

f. any other act, notification or communication relating to this Charter.

In witness whereof the undersigned, being duly authorised thereto, have signed this Charter.

Done at Strasbourg, this 15th day of October 1985, in English and French, both texts being equally authentic, in a single copy which shall be deposited in the archives of the Council of Europe. The Secretary General of the Council of Europe shall transmit certified copies to each member State of the Council of Europe.

DOCUMENT OF THE COPENHAGEN MEETING
OF THE CONFERENCE ON THE HUMAN DIMENSION
OF THE CSCE

The representatives of the participating States of the Conference on Security and Cooperation in Europe (CSCE), Austria, Belgium, Bulgaria, Canada, Cyprus, Czechoslovakia, Denmark, Finland, France, the German Democratic Republic, the Federal Republic of Germany, Greece, the Holy See, Hungary, Iceland, Ireland, Italy, Liechtenstein, Luxembourg, Malta, Monaco, the Netherlands, Norway, Poland, Portugal, Romania, San Marino, Spain, Sweden, Switzerland, Turkey, the Union of Soviet Socialist Republics, the United Kingdom, the United States of America and Yugoslavia, met in Copenhagen from 5 to 29 June 1990, in accordance with the provisions relating to the Conference on the Human Dimension of the CSCE contained in the Concluding Document of the Vienna Follow-up Meeting of the CSCE.

The representative of Albania attended the Copenhagen Meeting as observer.

The first Meeting of the Conference was held in Paris from 30 May to 23 June 1989.

The Copenhagen Meeting was opened and closed by the Minister for Foreign Affairs of Denmark.

At the Copenhagen Meeting the participating States held a review of the implementation of their commitments in the field of the human dimension. They considered that the degree of compliance with the commitments contained in the relevant provisions of the CSCE documents had shown a fundamental improvement since the Paris Meeting. They also expressed the view, however, that further steps are required for the full realization of their commitments relating to the human dimension.

In order to strengthen respect for, and enjoyment of, human rights and fundamental freedoms, to develop human contacts and to resolve issues of a related humanitarian character, the participating States agree on the following:

IV

(30)   The participating States recognize that the questions relating to national minorities can only be satisfactorily resolved in a democratic political framework based on the rule of law, with a functioning independent judiciary. This framework guarantees full respect for human rights and fundamental freedoms, equal rights and status for all citizens, the free expression of all their legitimate interests and aspirations, political pluralism, social tolerance and the implementation of legal rules that place effective restraints on the abuse of governmental power.

They also recognize the important role of non-governmental organizations, including political parties, trade unions, human rights organizations and religious groups, in the promotion of tolerance, cultural diversity and the resolution of questions relating to national minorities.

They further reaffirm that respect for the rights of persons belonging to national minorities as part of universally recognized human rights is an essential factor for peace, justice, stability and democracy in the participating States.

(31)   Persons belonging to national minorities have the right to exercise fully and effectively their human rights and fundamental freedoms without any discrimination and in full equality before the law.

The participating States will adopt, where necessary, special measures for the purpose of ensuring to persons belonging to national minorities full equality with the other citizens in the exercise and enjoyment of human rights and fundamental freedoms.

(32)   To belong to a national minority is a matter of a person's individual choice and no disadvantage may arise from the exercise of such choice.

Persons belonging to national minorities have the right freely to express, preserve and develop their ethnic, cultural, linguistic or religious identity and to maintain and develop their culture in all its aspects, free of any attempts at assimilation against their will. In particular, they have the right
(32.1) - to use freely their mother tongue in private as well as in public;
(32.2) - to establish and maintain their own educational, cultural and

religious institutions, organizations or associations, which can seek voluntary financial or other contributions as well as public assistance, in conformity with national legislation;

(32.3) - to profess and practise their religion, including the acquisition, possession and use of religious materials, and to conduct religious educational activities in their mother tongue;

(32.4) - to establish and maintain unimpeded contacts among themselves within their country as well as contacts across frontiers with citizens of other States with whom they share a common ethnic or national origin, cultural heritage or religious belief;

(32.5) - to disseminate, have access to and exchange information in their mother tongue;

(32.6) - to establish and maintain organizations or associations within their country and to participated in international non-governmental organizations.

Persons belonging to national minorities can exercise and enjoy their rights individually as well as in community with other members of their group. No disadvantage may arise for a person belonging to a national minority on account of the exercise or non-exercise of any such rights.

(33)   The participating States will protect the ethnic, cultural, linguistic and religious identity of national minorities on their territory and create conditions for the promotion to that effect after due consultations, including contacts with organizations or associations of such minorities, in accordance with the decision-making procedures of each State.

Any such measures will be in conformity with the principles of equality and non-discrimination with respect to the other citizens of the participating State concerned.

(34)   The participating States will endeavour to ensure that persons belonging to national minorities, notwithstanding the need to learn the official language or languages of the State concerned, have adequate opportunities for instruction of their mother tongue or in their mother tongue, as well as, wherever possible and necessary, for its use before public

authorities, in conformity with applicable national legislation.

In the context of the teaching of history and culture in educational establishments, they will also take into account the history and culture of national minorities.

(35)   The participating States will respect the right of persons belonging to national minorities to effective participation in public affairs, including participation in the affairs relating to the protection and promotion of the identity of such minorities.

The participating States note the efforts undertaken to protect and create conditions for the promotion of the ethnic, cultural, linguistic and religious identity of certain national minorities by establishing, as one of the possible means to achieve these aims, appropriate local or autonomous administrations corresponding to the specific historical and territorial circumstances of such minorities and in accordance with the policies of the State concerned.

(36)   The participating States recognize the particular importance of increasing constructive co-operation among themselves on questions relating to national minorities.   Such co-operation seeks to promote mutual understanding and confidence, friendly and good-neighbourly relations, international peace, security and justice.

Every participating State will promote a climate of mutual respect, understanding, co-operation and solidarity among all persons living on its territory, without distinction as to ethnic or national origin or religion, and will encourage the solution of problems through dialogue based on the principles of the rule of law.

(37)   None of these commitments may be interpreted as implying any right to engage in any activity or perform any action in contravention of the purposes and principles of the Charter of the United Nations, other obligations under international law or the provisions of the Final Act, including the principle of territorial integrity of the States.

(38)   The participating States, in their efforts to protect and promote the rights of persons belonging to national minorities, will fully respect their undertakings under existing human rights conventions and other relevant

conventions, if they have not yet done so, including those providing for a right of complaint by individuals.

(39)   The participating States will co-operate closely in the competent international organizations to which they belong, including the United Nations and, as appropriate, the Council of Europe, bearing in mind their on-going work with respect to questions relating to national minorities.

They will consider convening a meeting of experts for a thorough discussion of the issue of national minorities.

(40)   The participating States clearly and unequivocally condemn totalitarianism, racial and ethnic hatred, anti-semitism, xenophobia and discrimination against anyone as well as persecution on religious and ideological grounds. In this context, they also recognize the particular problems of Roma (gypsies).

They declare their firm intention to intensify the efforts to combat these phenomena in all their forms and therefore will

(40.1) - take effective measures, including the adoption, in conformity with constitutional systems and their international obligations, of such laws as may be necessary, to provide protection against any acts that constitute incitement of violence against persons or groups based on national, racial, ethnic or religious discrimination, hostility or hatred, including anti-semitism;

(40.2) - commit themselves to take appropriate and proportionate measures asures to protect persons or groups who may be subject to threats or acts of discrimination, hostility or violence as a result of their racial, ethnic, cultural, linguistic or religious identity, and to protect their property;

(40.3) - take effective measures, in conformity with their constitutional systems, the national, regional and local levels to promote understanding and tolerance, particularly in the fields of education, culture and information;

(40.4) - endeavour to ensure that the objectives of education include special attention to the problem of racial prejudice and hatred and to the development of respect for different civilizations and cultures;

(40.5) - recognize the right of the individual to effective remedies and endeavour to recognize, in conformity with national legislation, the right of interested persons and groups to initiate and support complaints against acts of discrimination, including racist and xenophobic acts;

(40.6) - consider adhering, if they have not yet done so, to the international instruments which address the problem of discrimination and ensure full compliance with the obligations therein, including those relating to the submission of periodic reports;

(40.7) - consider, also, accepting those international mechanisms which allow states and individuals to bring communications relating to discrimination before international bodies.

V

(41)   The participating States reaffirm their commitment to the human dimension of the CSCE and emphasize its importance as an integral part of a balanced approach to security and co-operation in Europe. They agree that the Conference on the Human Dimension of the CSCE and the human dimension mechanism described in the section on the human dimension of the CSCE of the Vienna Concluding Document have demonstrated their value as methods of furthering their dialogue and co-operation and assisting in the resolution of relevant specific questions. They express their conviction that these should be continued and developed as part of an expanding CSCE process.

(42)   The participating States recognize the need to enhance further the effectiveness of the procedures described in paragraphs 1 to 4 of the section on the human dimension of the CSCE of the Vienna Concluding Document and with this aim decide:

(42.1) - to provide in as short a time as possible, but no later than four weeks, a written response to requests for information and to representations made to them in writing by other participating States under paragraph 1;

(42.2) - that the bilateral meetings, as contained in paragraph 2, will take place as soon as possible, as a rule within three weeks of the date of the request;

(42.3) - to refrain, in the course of a bilateral meeting held under paragraph 2, from raising situations and cases not connected with the subject of the meeting, unless both sides have agreed to do so.

(43)   The participating States examined practical proposals for new measures aimed at improving the implementation of the commitments relating to the human dimension of the CSCE.   In this regard, they considered proposals related to the sending of observers to examine situations and specific cases, the appointment of rapporteurs to investigate and suggest appropriate solutions, the setting up of a Committee on the Human Dimension of the CSCE, greater involvement of persons, organizations and institutions in the human dimension mechanism and further bilateral and multilateral efforts to promote the resolution of relevant issues.

(44)   The representatives of the participating States express their profound gratitude to the people and Government of Denmark for the excellent organization of the Copenhagen Meeting and the warm hospitality extended to the delegations which participated in the Meeting.

(45)   In accordance with the provisions relating to the Conference on the Human Dimension of the CSCE contained in the Concluding Document of the Vienna Follow-up Meeting of the CSCE, the third Meeting of the Conference will take place in Moscow from 10 September to 4 October 1991.

Copenhagen, 29 June 199

CSCE HIGH COMMISSIONER ON NATIONAL MINORITIES

(I) The participating States decide to establish a High Commissioner on National Minorities

Mandate

(2)   The High Commissioner will act under the aegis of the CSO and will thus be an instrument of conflict prevention at the earliest possible stage.

(3)   The High Commissioner will provide "early warning" and, as appropriate, "early action" at the earliest possible stage in regard to tensions involving national minority issues which have not yet developed beyond an early warning stage., but, in the judgement of the High Commissioner, have the potential to develop into a conflict within the CSCE area, affecting peace, stability or relations between participating States, requiring the attention of and action by the Council or the CSO.

(4)   Within the mandate, based on CSCE principles and commitments, the High Commissioner will work in confidence and will act independently of all parties   directly involved in the tensions.

(5a)   The High Commissioner will consider national minority issues occurring in the State of which the High Commissioner is a national or a resident, or involving a national minority to which the High Commissioner belongs, only if all parties directly involved agree, including the State concerned.

(5b) The High Commissioner will not consider national minority issues insituations involving organized acts of terrorism.

(5c)   Nor will the High Commissioner consider violations of CSCE commitments with regard to an individual person belonging to a national minority.

(6) In considering a situation, the High Commissioner will take fully into account the availability of democratic means and international instruments to respond to it, and their utilization by the parties involved.

(7) When a particular national minority issue has been brought to the attention of the CSO, the involvement of the High Commissioner will require a request and a speciflc mandate from the CSO.

Profile, appointment, support

(8) The High Commissioner will be an eminent international personality with long-standing relevant experience from whom an impartial performance of the function may be expected.

(9) The High Commissioner will be appointed by the Council by consensus upon the recommendation of the CSO for a period of three years which may be extended for one further term of three years only.

(10) The High Commissioner will draw upon the facilities of the ODIHR in Warsaw and in particular upon the information relevant to all aspects of national minority questions available at the ODIHR.

Early warning

(11) The High Commissioner will:

(11a) collect and receive information regarding national minority issues from sources described below (see Supplement paragraphs (23)-(25));

(11b) assess at the earliest possible stage the role of the parties directly concerned, the nature of the
tensions and recent developments therein and, where possible, the potential consequences for peace and stability within the CSCE area;

(11c) to this end, be able to pay a visit in accordance with paragraph (17) and Supplement paragraphs (27)-(30) to any participating State and communicate in person, subject to the provisions of paragraph (25), with parties directly concerned to obtain first-hand information about the situation of national minorities.

165

(12)   The High Commissioner may during a visit to a participating State, while obtaining first-hand information from all parties directly involved, discuss the questions with the parties, and where appropriate promote dialogue, confidence and co-operation between them.

Provision of early warning

(13)   If, on the basis of exchanges of communications and contacts with relevant parties, the High Commissioner concludes that there is a prima facie risk of potential conflict (as set out in paragraph 3) he/she may issue an early warning, which will be communicated promptly by the Chairman-in-Office to the CSO.

(14)   The Chairman-in-Office will include this early warning in the agenda for the next meeting of the CSO. If a State believes that such an early warning merits prompt consultation, it may initiate the procedure set out in Annex 2 of the Summary of Conclusions of the Berlin Meeting of the Council ("Emergency Mechanism").

(15)   The High Commissioner will explain to the CSO the reasons for issuing the early warning.

Early action

(16)   The High Commissioner may recommend that he/she be authorized to enter into further contact and closer consultations with the parties concerned with a view to possible solutions, according to a mandate to be decided by the CSO. The CSO may decide accordingly.

Accountability

(17)   The High Commissioner will consult the Chairman-in-Office prior to a departure for a participating State to address a tension involving national minorities. The Chairman-in-Office will consult, in confidence, the participating State(s) concerned and may consult more widely.

(18)   After a visit to a participating State, the High Commissioner will provide strictly confidential reports to the Chairman-in-Office on the

findings and progress of the High Commissioner's involvement in a particular question.

(19) After termination of the involvement of the High Commissioner in a particular issue, the High Commissioner will report to the Chairman-in-Office on the findings, results and conclusions. Within a period of one month, the Chairman-in-Office will consult, in confidence, on the findings, results and conclusions the participating State(s) concerned and may consult more widely. Thereafter the report, together with possible comments, will be transmitted to the CSO.

(20) Should the High Commissioner conclude that the situation is escalating into a conflict, or if the High Commissioner deems that the scope for action by the High Commissioner is exhausted, the High Commissioner shall, through the Chairman-in-Office, so inform the CSO.

(21) Should the CSO become involved in a particular issue, the High Commissioner will provide information and, on request, advice to the CSO, or to any other institution or organization which the CSO may invite, in accordance with the provisions of Chapter III of this document, to take action with regard to the tensions or conflict.

(22) The High Commissioner, if so requested by the CSO and with due regard to the requirement of confidentiality in his/her mandate, will provide information about his/her activities at CSCE implementation meetings on Human Dimension issues.

Supplement

Sources of information about national minority issues

(23) The High Commissioner may:

(23a) collect and receive information regarding the situation of national minorities and the role of parties involved therein from any source, including the media and non-governmental organizations with the exception referred to in paragraph (25);

(23b) receive specific reports from parties directly involved regarding developments concerning national minority issues. These may include reports on violations of CSCE commitments with respect to national minorities as well as other violations in the context of national minority issues.

(24) Such specific reports to the High Commissioner should meet the following requirements:

- they should be in writing, addressed to the High Commissioner as such and signed with full names and addresses;

- they should contain a factual account of the developments which are relevant to the situation of persons belonging to national minorities and the role of the parties involved therein, and which have taken place recently, in principle not more than 12 months previously. The reports should contain information which can be sufficiently substantiated.

(25) The High Commissioner will not communicate with and will not acknowledge communications from any person or organization which practises or publicly condones terrorism or violence.

Parties directly concerned

(26) Parties directly concerned in tensions who can provide specific reports to the High Commissioner and with whom the High Commissioner will seek to communicate in person during a visit to a participating State are the following:

(26a) governments of participating States, including, if appropriate, regional and local authorities in areas in which national minorities reside;

(26b) representatives of associations, non-governmental organizations, religious and other groups of national minorities directly concerned and in the area of tension, which are authorized by the persons belonging to those national minorities to represent them.

Conditions for travel by the High Commissioner

(27)   Prior to an intended visit, the High Commissioner will submit to the participating State concerned specific information regarding the intended purpose of that visit. Within two weeks the State(s) concerned will consult with the High Commissioner on the objectives of the visit, which may include the promotion of dialogue, confidence and co-operation between the parties. After entry the State concerned will facilitate free travel and communication of the High Commissioner subject to the provisions of paragraph (25) above.

(28)   If the State concerned does not allow the High Commissioner to enter the country and to travel and communicate freely, the High Commissioner will so inform the CSO.

(29)   In the course of such a visit, subject to the provision of paragraph (25) the High Commissioner may consult the parties involved, and may receive information in confidence from any individual, group or organization directly concerned on questions the High Commissioner is addressing. The High Commissioner will respect the confidential nature of the information.

30)   The participating States will refrain from taking any action against persons, organizations or institutions on account of their contact with the High Commissioner.

High Commissioner and involvement of experts

(31)   The High Commissioner may decide to request assistance from not more than three experts with relevant expertise in specific matters on which brief, specialized investigation and advice are required.

(32)   If the High Commissioner decides to call on experts, the High Commissioner will set a clearly defined mandate and time-frame for the activities of the experts.

(33)   Experts will only visit a participating State at the same time as the High Commissioner. Their mandate will be an integral part of the mandate of the High Commissioner and the same conditions for travel will apply.

(34)   The advice and recommendations requested from the experts will be

submitted in confidence to the High Commissioner, who will be responsible for the activities and for the reports of the experts and who will decide whether and in what form the advice and recommendations will be communicated to the parties concerned. They will be non-binding. If the High Commissioner decides to make the advice and recommendations available, the State(s) concerned will be given the opportunity to comment.

(35)   The experts will be selected by the High Commissioner with the assistance of the ODIHR from the resource list established at the ODIHR as laid down in the Document of the Moscow Meeting.

(36)   The experts will not include nationals or residents of the participating State concerned, or any person appointed by the State concerned, or any expert against whom the participating State has previously entered reservations. The experts will not include the participating State's own nationals or residents or any of the persons it appointed to the resource list, or more than one national or resident of any particular State.

Budget

(37)   A separate budget will be determined at the ODIHR, which will provide, as appropriate, logistical support for travel and communication. The budget will be funded by the participating States according to the established CSCE scale of distribution. Details will be worked out by the Financial Committee and approved by the CSO.

(Helsinki, July 1992)

COMMISSION ON
SECURITY AND COOPERATION IN EUROPE

237 FORD HOUSE OFFICE BUILDING
WASHINGTON, DC 20515
(202) 225-1901

CSCE'S HIGH COMMISSIONER
ON NATIONAL MINORITIES
June 1993

The High Commissioner's Mandate

The CSCE created the post of High Commissioner on National Minorities at its July 1992 summit meeting in Helsinki, in response to the emergence of minority-related unrest as one of the main sources of conflict in Europe. Originally proposed by the Netherlands, the proposal received wide support as an innovative approach to national minority problems unleashed by the disappearance of superpower confrontation in Europe.

The High Commissioner is envisioned as an independent, unbiased individual of high stature, who can investigate national minority-related problems confidentially, before they reach crisis proportions. These are to be problems which, in the opinion of the High Commissioner, have the potential to develop into conflicts endangering international peace and security. The High Commissioner is empowered to gather information, including through visits, and to promote dialogue.1

Before beginning a visit, and again after consideration of an issue is completed, the High Commissioner must consult with the CSCE's Chair-in Office. If the issue is deemed to be of grave concern, an "Early Warning" of a threat to peace and security may be issued by the High Commissioner and discussed by the CSCE's Committee of Senior Officials (CSO), CSCE's central political body including representatives of all 53 participating states.2

Limitations

Some of the most innovative aspects of the original proposal for a High Commissioner were substantially watered down in response to individual state's concerns.

The High Commissioner may not become involved where armed conflict has already broken out or in areas already under consideration by the CSO, unless the permission of the CSO is given. Communication with or response to communications from organizations or individuals who practice or publicly condone terrorism is prohibited, as is involvement in situations "involving organized acts of terrorism."

The High Commissioner's mandate is constructed with emphasis on quiet diplomacy. This choice was deliberate in order to avoid pressuring governments or inflaming delicate situations, but it also deprives the High Commissioner of certain tools. Not only could this prestigious position exert considerable moral authority and pressure on governments and groups, but its potential for public diplomacy could be a boon for the little-known and less understood CSCE. Additionally, quiet diplomacy also justifies the strictly limited reporting to participating States envisioned by the mandates. The High Commissioner is only required to report to the CSCE's Chair-in-Office and through the Chair to the participating States; even a report to CSCE's bi-annual Human Dimension Implementation Meeting must be requested by the CSO.

Activities to Date

Former Dutch Foreign Minister Max van der Stoel was appointed the first High Commissioner in December 1992; his office began to function in January 1993, with premises donated by the Dutch government and a staff of three diplomats seconded from the Dutch, Polish and Swedish foreign ministries.

Van der Stoel chose for his first mission Estonia, Latvia and Lithuania, three small countries whose emancipation from Russian occupation left large Russian minorities with uncertain legal status. Estonia had previously requested and received a mission under the CSCE's Human Dimension Mechanism to consider whether its citizenship law met international standards; shortly after van der Stoel's visit, the CSCE placed a long-term mission in Estonia to help stimulate dialogue between the Estonian and Russian-speaking communities. Both in statements to press, government, and public in the three countries, and in a subsequent report presented to the CSO, van der Stoel chose to avoid direct criticism of any of the governments. His recommendations included pragmatic steps such as increasing availability of language instruction and the establishment of Ombudsmen or National Commissioners and other institutions to further dialogue and consideration of concrete problems.

Subsequently, van der Stoel turned to the prickly question of ethnic Hungarians in the newly-independent Slovak Republic, whose concerns had been a topic of much discussion in non-governmental circles. In his reporting to the CSO (subsequently made a publicly-available CSCE document, as were the Baltic reports), van der Stoel avoided any judgements on the situation of Hungarians in Slovakia.3 Instead, he developed a dual-sided approach which considered Slovaks in Hungary as well as Hungarians in Slovakia—to the surprise of experts, who have not considered Slovaks in Hungary as a problem of major proportions.

Acknowledging that the question needed further surveillance, van der Stoel proposed to the CSO a program of visits to Slovakia and Hungary by experts affiliated with his office - not to exceed four to each over two years. After some discussion, the plan was adapted by the CSO and will require reporting from the High Commission after each visit, with a final report at the end of the two-year period.

The CSO at its April 26-28, 1993 meeting also tasked the High Commissioner to study the problems of Roma (Gypsies) and their relevance to his mandate, in response to concern for the situation of Roma voiced in the report of the rapporteur mission to the newly admitted Czech and Slovak Republics. The High Commissioner visited Romania in June 1993, at the invitation of the Romanian government, and is working with Macedonia and Albania as well.

Early Assessment

While six months is evidently too short a period of time to pass judgment on the success of the High Commissioner's efforts toward early warning, conflict prevention, and problem solving it is not too soon to note

173

certain trends. Most significant are the results of the limitations imposed by the mandate. These include the High Commissioner's half constrained relations with participating States; the restrictions on his activity, limiting his ability to address many pressing minority issues; and the difficulty in coordinating his work with other initiatives.

First, the High Commissioner's independence effectively separates him from CSCE deliberations, activities, and structures, permitting a situation in which he traveled to Estonia precisely between a CSCE rapporteur mission and the establishment of a CSCE long duration mission to that country. One wonders whether some of the resources could not have been re-focused elsewhere, or at least better coordinated, particularly as the High Commissioner's mandate precludes activity in areas where the CSO is already engaged. Follow-up might be better coordinated with the participating States as well, increasing the role of the High Commissioner, and the profile of his issues, within CSCE's structures.

The limitations on High Commissioner activity are subject to some interpretation. The interpretations which van der Stoel has chosen to make so far lead, in the view of the Commission, to some unfortunate anomalies. For example, it is regrettable that the High Commissioner's office has remained entirely silent to date on the problems of Turkish Kurds, thus seeming to brands all Kurds with the terrorist label which prohibits High Commissioner activity, and displaying indifference to one of Europe's major human rights tragedies. Given the troubling handling of this serious human rights issues by the CSCE community to date, it seems to the Commission that the High Commissioner has abdicated what could be a leading role. Likewise, attention to the problems of Roma has thus far been limited to a study of their "relevance to the mandate of the High Commissioner," and that only after a decision by the CSO mandating him to do so. Arguments have been made that Roma issues do not "have the potential to develop into a conflict within the CSCE area affecting peace, stability or relations between participating States, requiring the attention of and action by the Council or CSO"4 While wars over Roma may well be unlikely, ignoring the problems of a group as badly mistreated and forgotten as the Roma casts favorable light neither on the High Commissioner nor on the participating States who have let it be known that Roma are not a fit topic for the High Cornmissioner's work.

A further consequence of the High Commissioner's limited mandate is the difficulty in connecting treatment of national minority issues with other economic or social problems that may increase or even underlie national minority tensions. For example, van der Stoel's initiatives cannot address the delays in Russian troop withdrawal that have done so much to poison ethnic relations in the Baltics; nor can they address general human rights shortcomings affecting all citizens of a given state. Thus far, van der Stoel's interpretation of his mandate has led him to function at a considerable mental as well as physical distance from CSCE's other activities. More efforts to be involved in CSCE activities relating to early warning and conflict prevention would improve CSCE's ability to address security comprehensively and to polish its image as a protector of human rights.

On a positive note, fears that the High Commissioner's separate role would further marginalize human rights issues within the CSCE have not materialized. Participating States' desire to scrutinize his work has ensured discussion of his activities in the CSO and the human dimension seminars of the CSCE Office for Democratic Institutions and Human Rights (ODIHR). His presentations at both types of meeting have been well-received (he delivered the keynote address at ODIHR's May 1993 Seminar on Case Studies on National Minorities Issues: Positive Results).

In his first report to the CSO, in April 1993, van der Stoel presented his proposals for follow-up in Estonia and Slovakia/Hungary that were mentioned above. Although they may be viewed as modest or disappointingly so, they were carefully prepared to be acceptable to the states concerned and were accepted without controversy. In the field of national minorities, this may in itself be regarded as something of an achievement. His success in visiting states and crafting reports which treat issues seriously without meeting vocal objections also casts a positive light on van der Stoel himself and the respect shown his post.

This being said, some might have hoped that the office of the High Commissioner would take a more aggressive approach. Van der Stoel has clearly chosen, however, to maximize his role as a governmental insider, slightly distanced from CSCE governments but acting on their behalf rather than as a voice in the wilderness. An early positive result is the acceptance he has won; more concretely, at least one country, Canada, has responded positively to his appeal for language teachers for Estonia.

As long as the High Commissioner remains such an "insider," it is particularly to be hoped that he can cooperate more broadly with CSCE structures to maximize the impact of CSCE's limited resources and to inject valuable human rights perspectives into as broad a spectrum of CSCE concerns as possible. The Commission looks forward to further developments, including the chance at the 1994 Budapest Review Conference to review and revise the High Commissioner's mandate in ways that would allow him to address more completely and openly the problems of minorities in CSCE countries.

For More Information

The mandate of the High Commissioner is printed in the Helsinki Document 1992; the decisions to name van der Stoel to the post and set up his office are appended to the decisions of the 18th CSO, December 11-13, 1992, and the Stockholm Meeting of the CSCE Council of Ministers, December 14-14, 1992. Analyses of the mandate and of his role include:

Conflict Management Group/Harvard Negotiation Project, Early Warning and Preventive Action in the CSCE: Defining the Role of the High Commissioner on National Minorities, Cambridge, MA: Conflict Management Group, 1993.

Staff of the Commission on Security and Cooperation in Europe, "The High Commissioner on National Minorities," in Beyond Process: The CSCE's Institutional Development, 1990-92, Washington, D.C.: The Commission on Security and Cooperation in Europe, 1992, pp. 27-28.

Hannie Zaal, "The CSCE High Commissioner on National Minorities," in The Helsinki Monitor, Utrecht: Netherlands Helsinki Committee, 1992, no. 4, pp. 33-37.

To contact the office of the High Commissioner:

CSCE High Commissioner on National Minorities
P.O. Box 20062
2500 EB The Hague
The Netherlands

Telephone: (31 70) 362 25 88
Fax: (31 70) 363 59 10

NOTES

1   The High Commissioners mandate is Section II of the Helsinki Document 1992: Challenges of Change.

2 CSCE's members include the United States and Canada and all the states of Europe and the former Soviet Union, except Macedonia, which has observer status. The "Federal Republic of Yugoslavia" (Serbia-Montenegro) has been suspended since July 1992.

3 The relevant decisions are available in the Journal of the 21st CSO, April 26-28, 1993. This and other CSCE documents referred to, including the High Commissioner reports, are available through the CSCE Secretariat in Prague, Czech Republic.

4   Section II, paragraph 3 of the 1992 Helsinki Document.

CENTRAL EUROPEAN INITIATIVE

CEI INSTRUMENT
for the protection of minority rights

The Member States of the Central European Initiative signatory hereto,

recognizing that the questions relating to national minorities can only be resolved satisfactorily in a truly democratic political framework which is based on the rule of law and guarantees full respect for human rights and fundamental freedoms, equal rights and status for all citizens,

reaffirming that the protection of national minorities concerns only citizens of the respective state, who will enjoy the same rights and have the same duties of citizenship as the rest of the population,

convinced that national minorities form an integral part of the society of the States in which they live and that they are a factor of enrichment of each respective State and society,

bearing in mind that a very effective remedy to achieve stability in the region are good relations between neighbours, and being conscious of the need to avoid any encouragement of separatist tendencies of national minorities in the region,

confirming that issues concerning the rights of persons belonging to national minorities are matters of legitimate international concern and consequently do not constitute exclusively an internal affair of the respective State,

considering that respect for the rights of persons belonging to national minorities, as part of universally recognized human rights, is an essential factor for peace, justice, stability and democracy in the States,

convinced that the international protection of the rights of persons belonging to national minorities, as enshrined in the present Instrument, does not permit any activity, which is contrary to the fundamental principles of international law and in particular of sovereignty, territorial integrity and political independence of States, recognizing the particular importance of increasing constructive co-operation among themselves on questions relating to national minorities, and that such co-operation seeks to promote mutual understanding and confidence, friendly and good-neighbourly relations, international peace, security and justice,

expressing their condemnation of aggressive nationalism, racial and ethnic hatred, anti-Semitism, xenophobia and discrimination against any person or group and of persecution on religious and ideological grounds

have agreed as follows:

ART. 1

States recognize the existence of national minorities as such, considering them integral parts of the society in which they live and guarantee the appropriate conditions for the promotion of their identity. For the purpose of this Instrument the term "national minority" shall mean a group that is smaller in number than the rest of the population of a State, whose members being nationals of that State, have ethnical, religious or linguistic features different from those of the rest of the population, and are guided by the will to safeguard their culture, traditions, religion or language.

ART. 2

To belong to a national minority is a matter of free individual choice and no disadvantage shall arise from the exercise or non-exercise of such a choice.

ART. 3

States recognize that persons belonging to national minorities have the right to exercise fully and effectively their human rights and fundamental freedoms, individually or in common with others, without any discrimination and in full equality before the law. Those persons shall be able to enjoy the rights foreseen by the present Instrument individually or in common with others and to benefit from the measures ensuring those rights.

ART. 4

States guarantee the right of persons belonging to national minorities to express, preserve and develop their ethnic, cultural, linguistic or religious identity and to maintain and develop their culture in all its aspects.

ART. 5

The adoption of special measures in favour of persons belonging to national minorities aimed at promoting equality between them and the rest of the population or at taking due account of their specific conditions shall not be considered as an act of discrimination.

ART. 6

States shall take effective measures to provide protection against any acts that constitute incitement to violence against persons or groups based on national, racial, ethnic or religious discrimination, hostility or hatred, including anti-Semitism;

ART. 7.

States recognize the particular problems of Roma (gypsies). They undertake to adopt all the legal administrative or educational measures as foreseen in the present Instrument in order to preserve and to develop the identity of Roma, to facilitate by specific measures the social integration of persons belonging to Roma (gypsies) and to eliminate all forms of intolerance against such persons.

ART. 8.

Without prejudice to democratic principles, States, taking measures in pursuance of their general integration policy, shall refrain from pursuing or encouraging policies aimed at the assimilation of persons belonging to national minorities against their will and shall protect these persons against any action aimed at such assimilation.

ART. 9.

In case of modification of administrative, judicial or electoral subdivisions States should take into account that such modifications, among other criteria, will respect the existing rights of the persons belonging to national minorities and the exercise of those rights. In any case, they should consult,

according to national legislation, with the populations directly affected
before adopting any modification in the matter.

ART. 10

Any person belonging to a national minority shall have the right to use his
or her language freely, in public as well as in private, orally and in writing.

ART. 11

Any person belonging to a national minority shall have the right to use his
or her surname and first names in his or her language and the right to
official acceptance and registration of such surname and names.

ART. 12

Whenever in an area the number of persons belonging to a national minority
reaches, according to the latest census or other methods of ascertaining its
consistency, a significant level, those persons shall have the right, wherever
possible, to use, in conformity with ~applicable national legislation, their
own language in oral and in written form, in their contacts with the public
authorities of the said area. These authorities may reply as far as possible, in
the same language.

ART. 13

In conformity with their national legislation States may allow, where
necessary through bilateral agreements with other interested States, in
particular with neighbouring States, the display of bilingual or plurilingual
local names, street names and other topographical indications in areas where
the number of persons belonging to a national minority reaches, according
to the latest census or other methods of ascertaining its consistency, a
significant level. The display
of signs, inscriptions or other similar information of private nature also in
the minority language should not be subject to specific restrictions, other
than those generally applied in this field.

ART. 14

Any person belonging to a national minority, exercising religious freedom, shall have the right to use his or her own language in worship, teaching, religious practice or observance.

ART. 15

Whenever the number of persons belonging to a national minority reaches, according to the latest census or other methods of ascertaining its consistency, the majority of the population in an area, States will promote the knowledge of the minority language among officers of the local and decentralized state administrative offices. Endeavours should be made to recruit, if possible, officers, who, in addition to the knowledge of the official language, have sufficient knowledge of the minority language.

ART. 16

States recognize the right of persons belonging to national minorities to establish and maintain their own cultural and religious institutions, organizations or associations, which are entitled to seek voluntary financial and other contributions as well as public assistance, in conformity with national legislation.

ART. 17

States recognize the right of persons belonging to a national minority to establish and maintain their own private preschools, schools and educational establishments and possibly obtain their recognition in conformity with the relevant national legislation. Such establishments may seek public financing or other contributions.

ART. 18.

Notwithstanding the need to learn the official language of the State concerned, every person belonging to a national minority shall have the right to learn his or her own language and receive an education in his or her own language. The States shall endeavour to ensure the appropriate types and levels of public education in conformity with national legislation, whenever in an area the number of persons belonging to a national minority, according to the latest census or other methods of ascertaining its consistency, is at a significant level. In the context of the teaching of history and culture in such public educational establishments, adequate teaching of history and culture of the national minorities should be ensured.

ART. 19.

States guarantee the right of persons belonging to a national minority to avail themselves of the media in their own language, in conformity with relevant State regulations and with possible financial assistance. In case of TV and radio in public ownership, the States will assure, whenever appropriate and possible, that persons belonging to national minorities have the right of free access to such media including the production of such programmes in their own language.

ART. 20.

States shall guarantee the right of persons belonging to national minorities to participate without discrimination in the political, economic, social and cultural life of the society of the State of which they are citizens and shall promote the conditions for exercising those rights.

ART. 21.

States shall allow persons belonging to a national minority to establish political parties.

ART. 22.

In accordance with the policies of the States concerned, States will respect the right of persons belonging to national minorities to effective participation in public affairs, in particular in the decision-making process on matters affecting them. Therefore, States note the efforts undertaken to protect and create conditions for the promotion of the ethnic, cultural, linguistic and religious identity of certain national minorities by adopting appropriate measures corresponding to the specific circumstances of such minorities as foreseen in the CSCE documents.

ART. 23

Every person belonging to a national minority, while duly respecting the territorial integrity of the State, shall have the right to have free and unimpeded contacts with the citizens of another country with whom this minority shares ethnic, religious or linguistic features or a cultural identity. States shall not unduly restrict the free exercise of those rights. Furthermore States will encourage transfrontier arrangements at national, regional and local levels.

ART. 24

Any person belonging to a national minority shall have an effective remedy before a national judicial authority against any violation of rights set forth in the present Instrument, provided that those rights are enacted in national legislation.

ART. 25

In any area where those who belong to a national minority represent the majority of the population, States shall take the necessary measures to ensure that those who do not belong to this minority shall not suffer from any disadvantage, including such that may result from the implementation of the measures of protection foreseen by the present Instrument.

ART. 26

None of these commitments shall be interpreted as implying any right to engage in any activity in contravention of the fundamental principles of international law and, in particular, of the sovereign equality, territorial integrity and political independence of States. Nothing in the present Instrument shall affect the duties related to persons belonging to national minorities as citizens of the States concerned. Persons belonging to national minorities will also respect, in the exercise of their rights, the rights of others, including those of persons belonging to the majority population of the respective State or to other national minorities.

ART. 27

This Instrument shall not prejudice the provisions of domestic law or any international agreement which provide greater protection for national minorities or persons belonging to them.

Budapest, 1994. November 15.

NGO DOCUMENTS

NGO DOCUMENTS

• International Institute For Ethnic Group Rights and Regionalism
(1978)

Draft of an International Convention

on the Protection of National or

Ethnic Groups or Minorities

The States Parties to the present Convention,

Regarding that the General Assembly of The United Nations in its Resolution no. 217 C (III) has declared not to be indifferent to the fate of Minorities,

Regarding Art. 27 of the International Covenant on Civil and Political Rights which provides for the protection of certain characteristics of persons belonging to ethnic, religious or linguistic minorities,

Appreciating the valuable work contained in the Special Report submitted to the Sub-Commission on the Prevention of Discrimination and Protection of Minorities in the Study UN-Doc. E/CH.4/Sub.2/384,

Regarding Art. 1 of the UN Convention relating to the Elimination of all forms of Racial Discrimination which includes in its concept of Race also the concept of ethnic groups and protects them and their members against all forms of racial discrimination,

Welcoming Art. 1 of the Human Rights Covenants recognizing the right of all peoples to self-determination and its application to all peoples under foreign occupation and colonial domination,
Regarding regional instruments on Human Rights, in particular Art. 14 of the European Convention on Human Rights which guarantees for everyone belonging to a national minority the enjoyment of the human rights and fundamental freedoms recognized in these instruments,

Welcoming the efforts made at the World Conference to combat Racism and Racial Discrimination (held at Geneva August 14-25 1978) for promoting the idea of the protecion of minorities against discrimination;

Considering the fact that the prevention of discrimination against persons belonging to ethnic or national minorities or groups is already deprecated by other international instruments in different fields and by many constitutional provisions in different regions of the world

Considering, however, that no general inernational instrument relating to the protection of elhnic groups and minorities has been elaborated, so far

Taking into account, that many national or ethnic groups or minorities in different regions of the world are not yet recognized as legally existent,

Anxious to prevent in the future any further threat to international or national peace and security caused by racial hatred and struggles of ethnic groups or minorities against oppression, such as the world experienced between the two World Wars, by the policies of racist regimes, by forms of genocide and other gross violations of human rights and fundamental freedoms,

Aware that universal or even regional protection of national and ethnic groups or minorities depends primarily on the democratic, economic, social, cultural and political development in the different regions of the world and that therefore the system of protection of ethnic groups and minorities must be secured by appropriate international instruments,

Taking note of the UN bodies' attempts to draft an International Declaration on religious intolerance and discrimination on grounds of religious beliefs,

Considering it inappropriate, however, to draft rules for the protection of religious minorities and national or ethnic groups or minorities in one and the same instrument,

Have decided to adopt a system of measures aiming at the protection of national or ethnic groups or minorities which may be implemented by Member States, but should in any case be considered as a first step towards a State policy designed to construct a peaceful poly-ethnic national society for the benefit of internal and international peace and security in conformity

187

with the principles of the UN Charter and the statutes of regional intergovernmental organizations,

Realizing that the national or ethnic groups or minorities and their members, having duties towards other ethnic groups and minorities and their members, are under a responsibility to refrain from ethnic prejudice and to strive for ethnic tolerance,

Agree upon the following sections and articles which thereby constitute elements of Human Rights and Fundamental Freedoms.

Section I: General Principles

Art. 1: Every national or ethnic group or minority has, on an international as well as on a national level, the inalienable right to be recognized as a national, ethnic and cultural entity and must be granted the right to be recognized as such in accordance with the provisions of the present Convention.

Art. 2: National or ethnic groups or minorities having the character of entities possess the inalienable right to their own ethnic and cultural identity and to self-determination within the framework of the present Convention.

Art. 3: Every member of a national or ethnic group or minority has the right to use his own language or dialect in private, in all social, economic and similar relations, and in public, notwithstanding the legal position of his group or minority.

Art. 4: National or ethnic groups or minorities are free to pursue their economic, social, and cultural development and may not be discriminated against for reasons connected either directly or indirectly with these activities.

Art. 5: National and ethnic groups and minorities have a right to a legal and social environment favourable to their legitimate aspiration.

Art. 6: The physical character as well as the demographic composition of a territory in which national or ethnic groups or minorities are living must not be changed without legitimate cause and the consent of those concerned.

Art: 7: The State must not undertake, support or favour a policy of artificial or enforced assimilation.

Art. 8: Genocide against national or ethnic groups or minorities is a crime against humanity.

Art. 9: Mass-expulsions of members of national or ethnic groups or minorities have to be considered as genocide; involuntary transfers of members of national or ethnic groups or minorities within or outside the borders of a State Party to this Convention are not permitted for any reasons whatsoever.

Art. 10: Nobody may be denied the right to assimilate voluntarily with the majority of the population of the State of which he is a national.

Section II: The Recognition of Groups, Prevention of Discrimination, and Measures of Protection in general

Art. 11: 1. The States Parties to this Convention recognize national or ethnic groups or minorities within their jurisdiction. They recognize furthermore the right of persons freely to join such groups or minorities.

2. A national or ethnic group or minority in the sense of the present Convention exists if a number of nationals of the given State, being in numerically inferior, non dominant position, and possessing ethnic or linguistic characteristics differing from the rest of the population, show, if only implicitly, a sense of solidarity with a view towards preserving their culture, traditions, or language and possessing also an adequate representation, asks for legal recognition as a national or ethnic group or minority.

3. A group or minority recognized according to § 2 may appeal for recognition by the UN or, if it so desires, by a relevant regional intergovernmental organization. As to the criteria according to which recognition is granted to such a body, UN-ECOSOC or the given regional inter-governmental organization decide, guided by the principles laid down in § 2. By force of recognition, the minority or group receives a special consultative status within the UN-ECOSOC or the respective

intergovernmental organization.

Art. 12:1. National or ethnic groups or minorities are guaranteed their political, cultural, economic, and social development on the basis of non-discrimination by the State. The authorities will also take appropriate steps to discourage discrimination on the part of the general population. Members of a minority or group may not be discriminated against either in fact or in law, in the enjoyment of human rights, especially those guaranteed by the UN Covenant on Social, Economic, and Cultural, and on Civil and Political Rights; the provisions of the UN Covenant on the Elimination of all forms of Racial Discrimination have likewise to be applied.

3. Members of a minority or group must not be obliged to render military service outside the territory in which the group resides unless in times of war or of public emergencies which do not involve specific interests of the minority or group concerned.

Art. 13: 1. The protection of a national or ethnic minority or group may be organized on a national or international level or on both levels. The kind, range and scope of the protection depends on the freely expressed will of the members of the minority group, on its demographic distribution as well as on international obligations of the given State.

2. The main kinds of protection on a national level are the following:

a) the right to self-determination as expressed in the UN Declaration of Principles of International Law on Friendly Relations and Cooperation among States in accordance with the Charter of the UN (GA Res. 2625 (XXV);
b) cultural autonomy;
c) linguistic autonomy;
d) participation in legislative, administrative, and/or judicial processes and decisions;
e) distribution of public funds for the promotion of the economic, cultural, and social development of the minority or group;
f) adequate competence to dispose of, and to use the natural resources located in the territory wherein the minority resides;
g) the right to economic, social, and cultural development based on the guarantees laid down in the UN Covenant on Economic, Social, and Cultural Rights.

3. The main kinds of protection on an international level are the following:
a) adjudication of a given type of self-determination on appeal of an internationally recognized minority or group by the General Assembly of the UN or the competent organ of a regional intergovernmental organization:
b) enquiry, mediation and conciliation in a conflict about group-protection between States at the request of a State, or in a conflict between a State and a group or minority at the request of the latter, on the basis of a Resolution of the UN General Assembly or of the competent organ of a regional intergovernmental organization the procedure has to follow the rules determined as a model procedure by the Hague Convention No. VII of 1907 (Peaceful Settlement of Disputes);
c) arbitration and/or judicial decision on an alleged violation of international instruments concerning group protection; the procedure to follow the rules of the aforementioned Hague Convention of 1907; competence for judicial decisions shall be assigned primarily to a Court or Commission of Human Rights established by an international regional agreement or, provided that no such agreement exists, to the International Court of Justice;
d) enquiry, mediation, conciliation, arbitration and/or judicial settlement on an alleged violation of rules of the national law written or unwritten serving directly or indirectly towards the application of an international instrument of obligation concerning group-protection; the procedure to follow the regulation of lit..
(e) international recognition of the minority or group by the UN or by a regional intergovernmental organization in the sense of Art. 11 § 3.

Section III: The Right of Self-Determination

Art. 14: The modes of implementing the right of self-determination of a national or ethnic minority or group consist in the right to
a) freely secede from the given State in order to establish a sovereign and independent State, or to associate with or integrate into an independent State, in the second alternative with the consent of the receiving State;
b) free emergence into any other political status (for instance, territorial autonomy, self-government, personal autonomy or any other agreed arrangement within the framework of the State directly concerned) or
c) freely form legislative and/or administrative regional or local autonomy within the framework of the State directly concerned.

Art. 15:1. The type of self-determination mentioned in Art. 14 lit. a) may only be granted to national or ethnic minorities or groups living in territories bordering on the receiving State or separated from it by the sea or a sea belt, provided that the secession has been voted upon in a free plebiscite by the majority of the population residing within the respective territory; the State may not hinder the free expression of the will to make use of the right of self-determination. The State may contribute to the exercise of the right of self-determination. The implementation of that right may, in agreement with the given State, be supervised by an intergovernmental organization .

2. Should the State not be inclined to recognize the group's right to self-determination in the sense of § 1, the group may appeal to the UN General Assembly or a competent regional intergovernmental organization for a decision on the legitimacy of its claim to self-determination.

3. If a minority or group is not accorded the right to self-determination in the sense of § 1, the State concerned may, by agreement with the duly authorized representatives of the minority or group, or by plebiscite, make arrangements in the sense of Art. 14, lit. b) or c).

Art. 16: The types of self-determination mentioned in Art. 14, lit. b) and c), may also be granted if, in a given territory of the State, nationals reside possessing ethnic or linguistic characteristics differing from the rest of the population and showing, if only implicitly, a sense of solidarity with a view towards preserving their culture, traditions, or language and also possessing an adequate representation, ask for such an arrangement.

Section IV: Other Forms of Autonomy

Art. 17: Every national or ethnic minority or group has the right to preserve its own cultural goods, whatever their form (archives, museums, libraries, monuments, theatres, orchestras, cultural institutions of any other kind etc.) may be, and to administer them by means of cultural autonomy. Every minority or group has the right to freedom of expression and therefore the right to establish its own information and press service.

Art. 18: A national or ethnic minority or group has the right to use a specific wireless and television channel - channels to be accorded in concordance with pertinent international understandings - and to transmit any program in its own language at adequate times.

Art. 19: Cultural autonomy consists further in an educational system providing instruction on all educational levels in the language of the group. Every child belonging to the group has the right to this education, provided the persons responsible for his education are willing to make use of this right. The relevant curricula have to take into account the needs of the group as well as the principles enshrined in the State's Constitution. Diplomas and certificates issued by the educational institutions of the group shall have public recognition. The provisions of the UNESCO Convention against Discrimination in Education of 1960 shall be applied respectively.

Art. 20: 1. Linguistic autonomy consists in facilitating the use of the mother tongue, before administrative and judicial authorities. If more than a certain percentage of the inhabitants of a certain judicial or administrative district - the percentage to be fixed by agreement between the competent State authorities and the representatives of the relevant minority or group - belong to one or more national or ethnic minority or group, their languages have to be recognized as official languages. Districts may not be delimited in a way so as to prevent the realization of this right. In cases of linguistic autonomy, topographic signs have to bear bi- or multilingual inscriptions.
2. This linguistic autonomy should particularly be observed with regard to the rights of personal liberty, of fair trial and in all matters of social welfare.
3. If necessary, State authorities shall consider the possibility of applying ethnic criteria with regard to the assignments of posts, especially in regions where the group language is recognized as the official language. In areas where the group resides, a percentage of posts in the Public Service of the State, the provinces and communes - the percentage to be fixed by agreement between the competent State authorities and the representatives of the relevant minority or group - shall be made available to members of that minority or group.

Art. 21:1. A national of ethnic minority or group is entitled to an equitable share of the minority or group as well as its individual members, in the general economic and social progress of the country. Within the framework of national legislation, at the same time in observance of the overriding guarantees enshrined in the UN Covenant on Economic, Social and Cultural Rights, the State authorities are obliged to cooperate with the minority or group representatives to this end.
2. In any case, the right of national or ethnic minorities or groups to establish federations or trade unions on an ethnical basis, to control the application of the principle of non-discriminatory job reservation, and to

reserve jobs for members of the minority or group adequate to their job training, must be safeguarded.

Section V: Group Representation and Group Behaviour

Art. 22: 1. National or ethnic minorities or groups may be represented by political parties or by corporations of a cultural or social nature.
2. These parties or corporations must have representative democratic organs, at regular time-intervals freely elected; in any case, for the determination of these organs, the principles governing the nomination, appointment, or election, as well as the duration of office of the principal organs of the State or its leading party must be applied respectively.

Art. 23: For the fulfilment of the tasks connected with the preservation and development of the characteristics of resident national or ethnic minorities or groups, the State has to give adequate material, and especially financial aid and assistance. In federal States, this applies also to their composite territorial units.

Art. 24: The State (in federal States their composite territorial units as well), the provinces and municipal bodies where national ethnic minorities or groups reside in considerable strength (the pertinent percentage to be fixed by agreement between the competent State authorities and the representatives of the relevant minority or group), may create Councils in order to render it possible for the groups to formulate and articulate their interests and desires, in particular with regard to the provisions laid down in the present Convention.
Art. 25: If, for reasons of insufficient numerical strength, national or ethnic minorities or groups cannot be represented in legislative bodies or administrative organs, or if self-determination or autonomy is not granted, the State shall provide for a sufficient number of national or ethnic representatives to be integrated into those bodies or organs in order to enable the minorities or groups to formulate and articulate their interests and desires. In matters where the principles of the present Convention are at stake or might come into jeopardy, it may be provided that no resolution may be passed nor any administrative decision be arrived at without the concurrence of the representatives of the minority or group.

Art. 26: Group representatives have the right to present the interests of the respective group before inter-governmental organizations; they have the right to present petitions in the name of the members of their group if individual rights or collective interests are alleged to be violated by public authorities.

Art. 27: The representation of group interests before national or international authorities shall be carried out in a manner excluding any instigation to individual or collective antipathy or hatred, or to violence against objects or persons. Representations made in conformity with these rules must in no case lead to repercussions on the group itself, their members or representatives or relatives or friends of these persons.

Art. 28: 1. National or ethnic minorities or groups owe loyalty towards the State in which they reside as long as the authorities of the State respect the principles set forth in the present Convention and do their best to enforce them. In no case may members of a group be discriminated against or expatriated because of their political activities connected with the representation or protection of national or ethnic collective interests or individual rights.
2. It may not be considered disloyal if representatives of a minority or group communicate with authorities of another State in matters concerning group interests, with regard to principles enshrined in the present Convention or in matters concerning bilateral agreements referring to group-protection, provided that members of the group belong to the people of the other State or that there exist cultural or traditional links between the group and the people of the other State.

Art. 29: With regard to international group protection (see Art. 12), the representation of a national or ethnic minority or group shall be given a legal status as to the claim for international recognition of the group (Art. 11 § 3), as to the right of self-determination (Arts. 14-16), as to the decision in conflicts between States and groups (Art. 13 § 3); representatives of groups shall be permitted to participate as legal representatives in cases concerning an alleged violation of human rights of a member of a group. Rules of procedure applied to international bodies shall be interpreted in this sense.

Section VI: Rules for International Implementation

Art. 30: The States Parties to the present Convention shall adapt their

195

respective laws and regulations with a view to bring them into harmony with the principles of the present Convention within two years after its entering into force.

Art. 31:1. All international conventions and instruments on cultural, economic, and social rights, on civil and political rights, as well as instruments relating to the friendly settlement of conflicts may be applicable to the prevention of racial discrimination in the field of human rights.
2. States Parties to the present Convention shall become Parties to the UN Convention on the Elimination of All Forms of Racial Discrimination.
3. The States Parties to the present Convention undertake to use their influence, both individually and jointly, towards the adaption of the Statutes of those inter-governmental organizations whose membership they possess, with regard to human rights in the sense of the principles laid down in the present Convention, in particular with regard to its Sections III and IV and its Art. 28.
4. States Parties to the present Convention agree that the procedure set up in ECOSOC Resulution "Procedure for dealing with communications relating to violations of human rights and fundamental freedoms" (Res. 1503 (XLVIII)) should be applied respectively for the purposes of the present Convention.

Art. 32:1. The States Parties to the present Convention shall appoint a High Commissioner for the Protection of the Rights of National or Ethnic Minorities or Groups whose functions are determined by a Special Statute annexed to the present Convention. The decision of the States Parties to the present Convention to appoint the High Commissioner has to be made unanimously.
2. If no agreement is reached as to the appointment of the High Commissioner, that States Parties to the present Convention will submit a list of at least three names to the UN Secretary General with the request to propose one of these persons for High Commissioner. The States Parties to the present Convention undertake to appoint the UN Secretary-General's nominee.

Section VII: Religious Minorities

Art. 33: The States Parties to the present Convention undertake to concentrate their efforts on the elaboration of international instruments on the protection of religious groups and minorities whose member rights are recognized in Art. 27 of the International Covenant on Civil and Political Rights.

Section VIII: Regional Arrangements

Art. 34: 1. The provisions of Art. 13, Art. 14 lit. c, Arts. 18-20 and Arts. 22-26 of the present Convention demand different forms of application in different regions of the world. These provisions should be implemented either by bilateral or by multilateral regional arrangement.
2. These agreements should take into account the annexed model-protocol about specific rights of ethnic groups and minorities.

Section IX: Concluding Provisions

Art. 35: For the purposes of the present Convention, Art. 2 § 3 and Arts. 4 and 5 of the International Covenant on Civil and Political Rights may be applied respectively.

Art. 36: National or international law more favourable to national or ethnic minorities or groups than are the provisions of the present Convention is not abrogated by the coming into force of the present Convention. In cases of disputes over this problem between States Parties to the present Convention, or between States Parties to the present Convention and international organizations, or between States Parties to the present Convention and nationally or internationally recognized minorities or groups, such a dispute may be decided upon by the International Court of Justice on the demand of one of the parties to the dispute.

Art. 37: Art. VI of the International Covenant on Civil and Political Rights has to be applied with regard to signatures and accessions, entry into force, extension of the Convention to federal States, amendments to the present Convention, notification, and authentic language.

Art. 38: States Parties to the present Convention are permitted to interpretative declarations only with regard to the ways and means of the intended application of the right of self-determination within their jurisdiction.

Art. 39. States Parties to the present Convention shall encourage bilateral and regional cooperating among themselves as well as between themselves and other interested States with regard to the rights and the protection of national or ethnic minorities or groups as outlined in the present Convention. Particularly, agreements shall be concluded on the exchange of lecturers, students, pupils and apprentices, on the nostrification of diplomas and certificates, on the exchange of information and experiences as well as the achievements of national or ethnic minorities or groups in cultural, educational, scientific and other fields of human endeavour.

Federal Union of European Nationalities

BASIC PRINCIPLES OF A RIGHT OF NATIONALITIES

Unanimously adopted by the 17th Congress of the FUEN
in its sitting at Abenra on 22nd May 1967

The universal Human Rights are established in the Universal Declaration of Human Rights of the United Nations and in the European Convention for the Protection of Human Rights and Fundamental Freedoms.

These rights shall be achievable for everybody.

Article 2 (1), of the Universal Declaration says in this regard:

"Everyone is entitled to all the rights and freedooms set forth in this Declaration, without distinction of any kind, such as race, colour, sex, language, religion, political or other opinion, national or social origin, property, birth or other status."

Article 14 of the European Convention declares:

"The enjoyment of the rights and freedoms set forth in this Convention shall be secured without discrimination of any ground such as sex, race, colour, language, religion, political or other opinion, national or social origin, association with a national minority, property, birth or other status."

The respect of human rights and fundamental freedoms is condition of a loyal attitude towards the State and the mutual respect of all its citizens and ethnic groups. In order to secure to national minorities resp. nationalities the rights set forth in the Declarations mentioned, the FUEN estimate that the following BASIC PRINCIPLES OF RIGHT OF NATIONALITIES be made valid law:

l) Everybody has the right freely to join a national minority resp. nationality. The States are engaged to create the political and social conditions for free adhesion. This adhesion must neither be challenged nor investigated.

2) The benefits of all civic and political rights must be granted to all citizens irrespective of their adhesion to a national minority resp. nationality.

3) Every member of a national minority resp. nationality has the right freely to use orally and in writing and to preserve his language. This also comprises the right to instruction and to religious services including instruction in religion in his own language. Every State is bound to acknowledge and protect this right of the national minority resp. nationality.

4) Every member of a national minority resp. nationality has in his native soil the right to deal with all representative assemblies, courts and authorities directly in his own language, orally as well as in writing.

5) Moreover has every member of a national minority resp. nationality the right to freedom of movement as well as to remain in his region of origin. Members of a national minority resp. nationality must not - if they are public officers - be transferred to areas outside the region of their nationality without their approval.

6) Every national minority resp. nationality has the inviolable and inalienable right of protection, maintenance and development of its characteristics. This right is general and not limited to such groups which are recognized by international agreements.

7) Every national minority resp. nationality has the right to associate. It has the right to cultural autonomy comprising its own management of schools and in the field of the church. The national minorities resp. nationalities must for these purposes receive an equitable share of the public grants. Every national minority resp. nationality has also the right to equitable time in radio and television.

8) The population of a territory in a State which mainly consists of a national minority resp. nationality should be granted the right of territorial autonomy and to regional legislative power. The territorial autonomy shall be guaranteed a proportionate share of the public grants.

9) Every national minority resp. nationality has the right to adequate

representation in parliaments as well as in all legislative and administrative boards. Evasive representations should not be used against national minorities resp. nationalities.

10) If a national minority resp. nationality is domiciled in a State which adheres to a Community of States with supra-national authorities, it shall be entitled to a proportionate representation in the assemblies of the peoples in that community.

11) The organizations of the national minorities resp. nationalities are entitled to represent their own interests as well as those of their groups and their individual adherents. A national minority resp. nationality, the rights of which are affected by the State, can demand help and protection by lodging a complaint with national, European or international courts.

12) The States and communities of States are morally engaged to organize their economic conditions in that way which ensures that adherents of the national minorities resp. nationalities can find occupation in their own territory, and do not find themselves forced to emigrate into other territories of the State in order to find sufficient standard of living.

Nor should the economic development and industrialisation be used to submerge the territory of domicile of a national minority resp. nationality by means of labour forces of other nationalities.

REPUBLIC OF HUNGARY

OFFICE OF NATIONAL AND ETHNIC MINORITIES

ACT LXXVII OF 1993

ON THE RIGHTS OF NATIONAL AND ETHNIC MINORITIES

The Hungarian National Assembly]

— pursuant to the noblest traditions and values of Hungarian history,

— in the spirit of it commitment to the ideals of democracy and humanism,

— with the aim of promoting understanding and friendly co-operation among peoples and nations,

— moreover, being fully aware that the harmonious co-existence of national and ethnic minorities with the majority nation forms an integral part of international security,

declares that it considers the right of national and ethnic identity as a part of universal and human rights, and recognizes the specific individual and collective rights of national and ethnic minorities as fundamental civil rights and will assert these rights in the Republic of Hungary.

The totality of these rights is neither an endowment by the majority nation nor a privilege of minorities; the source of these rights does not derive merely from the numerical proportion of national and ethnic minorities, but on the basis of the respect for the individual freedom and for social peace their right to be different.

In declaring the ideals of equality and solidarity as well as the principles of active protection of minorities, taking into account the recognized universal moral and legal norms, the National Assembly is guided by its great esteem for minorities and respect moral and historical values, as well as for the consequent representation of the common vital interests of the minorities and the Hungarian nation.

The language, material and intellectual culture and historical traditions of the national and ethnical minorities, living on the territory of the Republic of Hungary and holding Hungarian citizenship, as well as any other particularity connected with their being minorities constitute a part of their individual and collectiv identity.

These are all particular values, the preservation, cultivation and enrichment of which do not only form a fundamental right of national and ethnic minorities, but are in the interest of the Hungarian nation and ultimately, of the community of states and nations as well

Considering that self-government constitutes the basis of a democratic system, the National Assembly treats the establishment of minority self-governments, their activities, and thereby the accomplishment of cultural autonomy, as one of the most important preconditions for the enforcement of specific minority rights.

Starting from the fact of historical co-existence, the National Assembly also intends the present act to ensure all those rights which are not only human rights of persons belonging to minorities or to minority communities as Hungarian citizens are entitled to, but are also political rights enabling them to preserve their national or ethnic identity. Relying on the principles included in the Helsinki Final Act, the present Act aims to create institutional bases necessary to enabling people to lead their life as national or ethnic minorities, including also the maintenance of unhindered and vivid relations with the respective mother countries or nations. In enacting the present Act, the National Assembly of the Republic of Hungary is guided by the intentions of creating a Europe without frontiers, of lessening and eliminating disadvantages originating in the minority life, and of the further development of the democratic institutional system needed to this end.

In order to achieve the above-mentioned purposes and to summarize the rights which individuals and communities belonging to national and ethnic minorities are entitled to, as well as to provide for the guarantee of predominance of these rights and regulation of the enforcement of them, the National Assembly - paying due attention to the principles laid down in the relevant provisions of international law, in the Charter of the United Nations, the Universal Declaration of Human Rights, the International Covenant of Civil and Political Rights, the Paris Charter for a New Europe, the European Convention on Human Rights, as well as in the Constitution of the Republic of Hungary - passes the following law:

CHAPTER I
Fundamental provisions

SECTION I

(1) The present Act covers all persons holding Hungarian citizenship and living on the territory of the Republic of Hungary, who consider themselves as national or ethnic minorities, as well as their communities.

(2) In the application of this Act, all those ethnic groups having been living on the territory of Hungary for at least one century, are to be regarded as national and ethnic minorities (henceforward: "minorities) who constitute a numerical minority within the population of the country, whose members hold Hungarian citizenship and who differ from the rest of the population in terms of their own mother tongue, cultures and traditions, and who prove to be aware of the cohesion, national or ethnic, which is to aim at preserving all these and at articulating and safeguarding the interests of their respective historically developed communities.

SECTION 2

The present Act is not to be applied to refugees, immigrants, permanent foreign residents and to the stateless persons.

SECTION 3

(1) Minorities living in the Republic of Hungary share alike in the power of the people, that is, they are state-forming constituent elements

(Section 68 subsection (1) of the Constitution). Their culture form part of culture of Hungary.

(2) The right to national or ethnic identity is a basic human right which individuals and communities are equally entitled to.

(3)　Every minority has the right to exist and subsist as a national or ethnic minority.

(4)　Each minority community and each person belonging to any given minority has the right to live in their land of birth and to maintain unhindered relations with their motherland. The right to motherland entails the freedom and protection of maintaining relations not only with one's birth-place, but also with the dwelling place and homeland of one's parents, fosterers, and ancestors, as well as with the country of origin and her culture and traditions.

(5)　Any negative discrimination against minorities is prohibited by law.

SECTION 4

(1)　The Republic of Hungary prohibits any policy which

—aims at or results in the assimilation of a minority to the
　majority nation,
— is directed to alter the national or ethnic conditions of territories
　inhabited by minorities to the disadvantage of the community
　in question;
—is to harass a national or ethnic minority or persons
　belonging thereto, to aggravate their living conditions or to
　prevent them from exercising their rights;
—aims at any forceful expulsion or resettlement of a national or
　ethnic minority.

(2)　In its international relations, the Republic of Hungary will take a strong stand against any political endeavor which might lead to such consequences as specified in condition (1). It also strives to provide for protection against any policy of this kind through the means of international law and international agreements.

(3)　In marking out the borders of administrative units and constituencies

205

as well as in the elaboration of settlement- and economic development plans, including environmental protection, the Republic of Hungary will take into account the particular settlement conditions, relations, economic interests and the historically developed traditions of national or ethnic minorities.

SECTION 5

Minorities living in the Republic of Hungary have a constitutional right to organize self-government at both local and national level.

(2)   The basic task of these minority self-governments is to safeguard and represent the interests of minorities by performing the duties and exercising the tasks and sphere of authority as laid down by the present Act.

(3)   To promote the fulfillment of tasks referred to above, the present Act regulates the ways and means of establishing the mentioned self-governments, their rights and duties, operational conditions as well as their relations with the government agencies and other state authorities.

SECTION 6

The Republic of Hungary also assists the equality of rights to come into full display through legal measures taken to eliminate inequalities lines in chances (Constitution's Subsection (3) of Section 70\a).

CHAPTER II
Individual minority rights

SECTION 7

The acceptance and confession of belonging to a certain national or ethnic minority (henceforward: minority) is an exclusive and inalienable right of the individual. However, no one shall be obliged or forced to make a declaration of belonging to a minority group.

(2)   The right to national or ethnic identity and the acceptance and manifestation of belonging to a minority does not preclude the recognition

of dual or multiple ties.

SECTION 8

A person belonging to a minority has the right to confess his or her belonging to a minority anonymously and secretly on the occasion of national censuses.

SECTION 9

A person belonging to a minority has the right to equal chances in the political and cultural spheres, which the state is bound to promote through adequate measures taken to this effect.

SECTION 10

The participation of minority persons in public life shall not be restricted. Under the provisions of the Constitution, they have the right to establish associations, parties and other social organizations to articulate and safeguard their particular interest.

SECTION 11

Persons belonging to a minority have the right to observe minority traditions related to family, to keep up family relations, to observe family celebrations and the related religious ceremonies in their mother tongue, and to make claim to all this.

SECTION 12

(1) Anyone belonging to a minority has the right to freely choose one's own and one's children's first name, to have one's family name and first name registered according to the grammatical rules of one's mother tongue, and to have them so recorded in official documents within the bounds of the effective legal regulations. In the case of registering in non-Latin script, the simultaneous phonetic transcription of names in Latin characters as well is required.

(2) Upon request, registration and the issuing of other personal documents may also be bilingual - in pursuance of subsection (1).

SECTION 13

Persons belonging to a minority have the right
a)   to get acquainted with, cultivate, enrich and transmit their mother tongue, history, culture and traditions,
b)   to participate in education and any other cultural activity in the vernacular language,
c)   to have protection of their personal data related to their belonging to a minority as laid down by a separate Act.

SECTION 14

Persons belonging to a minority have the right to maintain relations both with the governmental and communal institutions of the mother countries or language nations and with minorities living in other countries.

CHAPTER III
Collective rights of minorities

SECTION 15

It is an inalienable collective right of minorities to preserve, cultivate strengthen and transmit their identity as a minority.

SECTION 16

Minorities have the right to cultivate and enrich their historical traditions and vernacular language, to preserve and increase their national culture, both material and spiritual.

SECTION 17

Minorities have the right to establish social organizations and self-governments at both national and local level.

SECTION 18

In pursuance of a separate Act, the Hungarian Radio and Television as public services are to provide for the regular production and broadcasting of programs for national and ethnic minorities.

(2)   On   territories   inhabited   by   minorities,   the   government promotes - through international agreements, if necessary - the reception of radio and television broadcasts from the mother country.

(3)   Minority communities have the right

a)   to take the initiative in creating conditions for education at kindergartens, primary and secondary schools, as well as in higher education in the   vernacular, or in both their vernacular and Hungarian language;
b)   to develop their own national network of educational, training, cultural and scientific institutions - within the bounds of the relevant laws.

(4)   Within the bounds of the Acts the Republic of Hungary will ensure the undisturbed arrangement of programs and observation of celebrations of minorities, as well as their right to preserve, cultivate, and perpetuate their architectural cultural and religious relics and traditions, and also their right to the free use of their symbols.

SECTION 19

Minorities and their organizations are entitled to develop and maintain wide-ranging and direct international relations.

SECTION 20

(1)   In a manner determined by a separate law, minorities have the right to be represented within the National Assembly.
(2)   The National Assembly is to elect the ombudsman of the rights of national and ethnic minorities. The related management and preparatory works are to be performed by the Office of the   Parliamentary Spokesman (Ombudsman). In other respects, the relevant provisions of Law LIX of 1993 on the Parliamentary Spokesman of Civil Rights (Ombudsman) are to be applied to the minority ombudsman as well.
(3)   The Minority Ombudsman is to take measures in issues corning under the ruling of the present Act.

CHAPTER IV
Self-governments of minorities

SECTION 21

(1)   In terms of the present Act, the individual minorities can organize local minority self-governments, other municipal minority self-governments, established directly or indirectly, in settlements (villages and towns) and in the districts of the capital city of Budapest and also   minority self-governments at the national level.

(2)   Election of citizens belonging to minorities as local representatives should take place under Law LXIV of 1990 on the Election of Local Government Representatives and Mayors amended by Section 64 of the present Act.

SECTION   22

A local   government   within   which   more   than   half   of   the representatives were elected as candidates of a national or ethnic minority may declare itself a minority local government.

(2)   If at least 30 per cent of representatives of a local government were elected as   candidates   of   one   and   the   same   minority, these representatives may form minority local governments   consisting   of   at least   three   persons   by each   minority   concerned   (henceforward: indirectly   formed   minority   local governments).

SECTION 23

Election of Local Government Representatives and Mayors

(1)   In accordance with sections 51 to 54 of Act LXIV of 1990 on the Election of Local Government Representatives and Mayors as amended by Section   64 of the present Act, voters may   establish minority local government through direct election (henceforward: directly formed minority local governments).

(2)   Bodies of directly formed minority local governments should consist of 3 (three) members in villages of less than 1300 inhabitants, 5 (five) members in those of more than 1300 inhabitants, 7 (seven) members of towns, and of 9 (nine) members in county-rank towns and in the districts of Budapest.

(3)A directly formed minority local government is to elect its leading officials by itself -according to rules laid down by the majority of the body.

(4)   That member of a directly formed minority local government who is not a representative of the local government through an election - held in accordance with Section 51 to 54 of Act LXIV of 1990 on the Election of Local Government Representatives and Mayors as amended by Section 64 of the present Act - may only become a member of the body of the directly formed minority local government.

(5) A minority in a given settlement may establish only one indirectly formed minority local government, or for lack of this, only one directly formed minority local government.

(6)   Minority local governments, formed either directly or indirectly, (henceforward together: minority local government) have the same tasks and sphere of authority as defined by the present Act.

(7)   An ombudsman in the local government of a settlement may only act as a representative of a minority, if the given minority to be represented by him or her does not have a directly formed minority local government.

SECTION 24

Provisions of the Act on Local Governments are to be applied, whenever applicable, to local governments of minority settlements and to minority local governments, unless otherwise stated in the present Act.
Duties and sphere of competence of local governments of minority settlements and minority local governments.

SECTION 25

A minority local government is a legal entity. Beyond the tasks and sphere of authority of local governments of settlements laid down in the respective Act, those of the local governments of minority settlements are governed by the present Act.

(2)   In the process of administering the public affairs of local interest, local governments of minority settlements are bound - in compliance with subsection (1) - to ensure the enforcement of the rights of the Hungarian population and other national or ethnic minorities forming a numerical minority in the given settlement.

SECTION 26

(1)   In any matter concerning the conditions of the minority, local governments of minority settlements and minority local governments may lodge an application with the head of the competent administrative agency or body, in which it may

a)   request information;
b)   make proposal(s);
c)   initiate measures to be taken;
d)   make objection to any practice or individual decision affecting the functioning of institutions and violating the rights of minorities, and may also initiate the alteration or withdrawal of the decision in question.

(2) The head of the administrative agency possessing the necessary competence is bound - in cases defined in section (1) - to give a substantial response to the appeal within 30 (thirty) days.

(3)   Should the head of the given agency or body not have the necessary competence or sphere of authority, he or she is bound to transmit the appeal to the competent agency or body within 3 (three) days.

SECTION 27

(1)   Within its own sphere of authority and within the bounds of decrees of the local government of settlement, the minority local government is to make decisions in the following matters:

a)   its organization and rules of procedure;
b)   its budget, final account, and the use of resources placed at its disposal by the local government;
c)   use of assets which are separated for this purpose from the assets of the local government of the settlement in accordance with

the provisions of the present Act;

d) its name and symbol(s), its decorations and the preconditions and rules for awarding those decorations;

e) local celebrations of the minority represented by it;

f) the sphere of protected monuments and memorial places, as well as local rules for their protection, within the bounds of the effective legal regulations.

(2) On the initiative of the minority local government, the body of representatives of the local government of the settlement is bound to determine the assets to be provided for use by the minority local government to ensure its proper functioning as defined by the related legal measures. These assets and funds shall be specified in detail.

(3) Within its sphere of authority the m- minority local government - within the limits of its resources available - may establish and maintain institutions, especially in such fields as

a) local public education,

b) local printed or electronic media,

c) cultivating traditions,

d) culture and general education.

(4) Within the limits of the available resources, it is authorized:

a) to establish and run enterprises and other economic organizations;

b) to announce competitions;

c) to raise foundations.

(5) In case a special decision by the local government of the given settlement is required to enable the minority local government to vernacular exercise its rights, the body of representatives of that local government is bound the put the related initiative of the minority local government on the agenda of its next session. Should the related decision fall within the competence of another local government agency, the latter shall make a decision on the issue in thirty days from the submittal of the initiative in question.

SECTION 28

The Mayor's Office, set up by the local government of the settlement is bound - in a way defined by the organizational and operational rules - to help the minority local governments with their work.

SECTION 29

(1)   Local government decrees on issues concerning the local public education, local mass media, cultivating of local traditions, culture, and the collective use of language which affect the minority population as such, shall only be passed by the body of representatives in agreement with the minority local government representing the population concerned.

(2)   The appointment of leaders of minority institutions and local government decisions affecting also the education of people belonging to minorities, require the consent of the minority local government concerned. For lack of a minority local government, the opinion of the local minority ombudsman or in the absence of such an official, the opinion of the local minority association should be taken into account.

(3)   Those being authorized to express opinion or consent are bound to state their position connected with issues outlined in sections (1) and (2) in thirty days from the submittal or reception of the related document under pain of forfeiture of right.

SECTION 30

(1)   Local governments of minority settlements and minority local governments may maintain relations with any other minority organization, association, and may also conclude cooperation agreement with them.

(2)   Minority organizations, institutions and associations may participate in state-funded competitions invited for the development of nationality culture, education, science, and so forth, on even terms with the local governments of minority settlements and minority local governments.

Minority self-government at the national level

SECTION 31

Minority self-government at the national (henceforward: national-level self-government) may be organized in pursuance of the related provisions of this law.

(2)   The national-level self-government is elected by minority electors. Minority electors are: every representative of a local governments, provided he or she was elected as a minority representative, representatives of the minority local governments, and the minority ombudsmen. In case the affected minority has neither a minority representative nor an ombudsman in the body of representatives of a local government, or the affected minority does not have a minority local government within the given settlement, the election of an elector may be initiated by three voters residing in the settlement, who confess to belong to that minority.

(3)   On the initiative of at least three voters belonging to one and the same minority, an electoral meeting shall be convoked.

SECTION 32

Electoral meeting is to be convoked by the local electoral committee. One session should be held for each national or ethnic minority, in which voters with residence in the settlement may participate. The place and date of the meeting shall be made public by notices.

Electoral meeting is to be held in 60 (sixty) days from the second round of the general election of representatives of local governments and mayors.

The meeting of inhabitants belonging to one and the same national or ethnic minority is only entitled to elect a minority elector. The electoral meeting has a quorum if at least 10 (ten) minority voters are present. Participants elect the electors by secret ballot, by simple majority vote with ballots based on the results of an open nomination process.

In any given settlement, one minority may only elect one elector, and an elector may take on only one such commission.

The fact that in the given settlements only voters with residence have participated in the election, is to be checked by the local electoral committee relying on the register voters complied by the local clerk (town-clerk or village notary).

SECTION 33

In 3 (three) days after electoral meetings local election committees impart the names of the electors elected by the electoral meetings and belonging to one and the same minority to the National Election Committee.

The National Election Committee shall convoke the electors meeting in 30 (thirty) days from the term determined in subsection (2) of Section 32.

One and the same national or ethnic minority is allowed to establish only one national self-government. Different national and ethnic minorities may form a common, associated national self-government.

SECTION 34

Members of the General Meeting of the national self-government are elected, by secret ballot, by the electors from among themselves, applying the relevant rules for the local "small-list" elections_ as laid down by the Act on the Election of Local Government Representatives and Mayors. All candidates, who have been supported by at least ten per cent of the electors, have to be entered into the ticket. The statutory meeting of the General Meeting has a quorum only if at least three-quarters of the elected electors are present.

Tasks and sphere of authority of the national self-government

SECTION 35

(1) The commission of the members of the General Meeting of the national self-government will last until the day of the first session of the New General Meeting.

The statutory meeting of the new General Meeting must be convoked in thirty days from the election of the General Meeting representatives.

(2) In case no new General Meeting has been elected, the

216

national self-government is to cease.

SECTION 36

(1) The national self-government is to represent and safeguard the interests of minorities represented by it at both national and local level. In the interest of creating the cultural autonomy of minorities, it may organize institutions and coordinate their functioning.

(2) The national-level self-government is a legal entity.

(3) In case the national self-government ceases to function, its property falls to the National and Ethnic Minority Fund (henceforward: Fund) according to subsection (3) Section 55 of this law. The Fund is bound to manage the property which has thus got into its hands and to see that it is properly preserved. If the discontinued national self-government is formed anew and resumes its functioning, the Fund is bound to return its property.

SECTION 37

The national self-government - within the bounds of the pertinent Acts - is to decide independently in such issues as
a)   its seat, and procedure;
b)   its budget, final and inventory;
c)   scope of its principal stock,
d)   its name and symbols;
e)   the national holidays of the minorities represented by it;
f)   its decorations and the preconditions and rules for their awarding;
g)   principles and manner of using the public service radio and television channels placed at its disposal;
h)   principles of using the public service radio and television program placed at its disposal;
i)   publication of press statements;
j)   establishment of its institutions, the organizational and operational rules of their maintenance and operation;
k)   maintaining of a theatre;
l)   creating of exhibition facilities in museums, forming and maintaining public collections of nation-wide coverage;
m)   maintaining of a special minority library;

n)   founding and maintaining of art and scientific institutes and publishing houses;

o)   maintaining of secondary schools and higher educational institutions of nation-wide coverage;

p)   establishing and maintaining a legal aid;

r)   as well as all other matters referred to its sphere of authority by Acts.

SECTION 38

(1)The national self-government:

a)   is to express its opinion on drafts of legal measures affecting the minorities as such it represents, including the decrees of the general assemblies of counties and the capital city;

b)   may request the administrative agencies to supply information on matters affecting the groups of minorities it represents; may submit proposals to those bodies; may initiate measures to be taken in matters falling within their competence;

c)   along with the competent and authorized state bodies, it is to participate in the professional supervision of the first, second and third level education of minorities represented by it.

(2)   The administrative agency requested according to point b) of subsection (1) is to proceed pursuant to subsections (2) and (3) of Section 26.

(3)   In the course of legislation concerning the maintenance and preservation of historical settlements and architectural monuments of the minority, the national self-government, while in case of passing a local governmental decree in the same matter, the minority local government has a right to express its opinion and consent. In the absence of minority local government, the local ombudsman of the minority, for lack of the latter, the local minority association is entitled to exercise this right.

(4)   In the elaboration of the core material of minority education - except higher education- the affected national self-government has the right to express its opinion and consent.

SECTION 39

Within its field of activity, the national self-government may invite competitions and found scholarships.

CHAPTER V
The local ombudsman of minorities

SECTION 40

(1)   On the strength of subsection (5) of Section 12 of Act LXV of 1990 on the local governments (henceforward: LGA), the local ombudsman of minorities (henceforward: ombudsman) is authorized:

(a)   inasmuch as he or she is not a representative himself or herself, to participate with the right of discussion in any session, including closed sessions, of the body of representatives, or of committees when discussing of those items on the agenda which concern minorities;

(b)   to propose the mayor or the chairman of the committee that a certain matter concerning the conditions of minorities - provided it falls within the competence of the body of representatives or the committee - be put on the agenda to be discussed;

(c)   to initiate that the body of representatives revise its decision affecting the conditions of minorities;

(d)   to require information from the mayor, the clerk (notary) and the chairman at the sessions of the body of representatives or committees on matters that fall within the competence of the local government and concern the situation of minorities;

(e)   to require the mayor or the clerk (notary) to supply him the information and administrative assistance necessary to perform his duties;

(f)   to initiate certain measures to be taken by the mayor, the clerk (notary) or by other competent officials in matters concerning the minorities;

(g)   to propose that in a certain matter concerning the minorities, the body of representatives apply to that agency or body which is competent in that particular matter according to subsection (1) of Section 101 of LGA.

219

(2) On the basis of an initiative taken in accordance with point b) of subsection (1), the mayor or the chairman of the committee is bound to submit the ombudsman's proposal to the next session of the body of representatives or of the committee. The body of representatives or the committee is to decide on the date of putting the given issue on the agenda as well as on the related preparatory work.

(3) If the ombudsman requests information from the mayor, the clerk (notary) or from the chairman of the committee at the session of the body of representatives or the committee, he should be given adequate answer either at that session or - in written form - in not more than fifteen days from that session.

(4) Upon his request, the ombudsman's contribution must be included in the minutes of the session, or - if he submitted it in written form - it should be attached to the minutes.

(5) The discussion of an issue concerning the conditions of minorities which was initiated in conformity with point b) of subsection (1) and put on the agenda according to subsection (2), may only be adjourned or removed from the agenda by the body of representatives if the ombudsman so requires.

(6) Prior to passing a local government decree affecting the rights and duties of minorities or to taking a certain measure affecting the situation of minorities in general, the competent local government agency or body shall ask for the opinion of the ombudsman.

SECTION 41

(1) Upon his request, the ombudsman must be relieved from doing his normal work by his employer for a period necessary to perform his or her duties in this capacity. His or her loss in income on this account shall be recovered by the body of representatives. On the basis of this complementary income, the ombudsman is entitled to social insurance provision as well.

(2) In the case of the ombudsman too, legal measures governing the reimbursement of expenses, payment of allowances or fees to counselors are to be applied.

(3)   Provisions included in subsections (1) to (2) do not affect the rights and duties connected with membership in the body of local government representatives, if the ombudsman is also a member of that body.

CHAPTER   VI
The cultural and educational self-government of minorities

SECTION   42

According to the present Act languages used by minorities in Hungary are as follows: Armenian, Bulgarian, Croatian, German, Gypsy (Romany and Bea), Greek, Polish, Romanian, Ruthenian, Serb, Slovak, Slovene, Ukrainian.

SECTION   43

(1)   The state considers the respective mother tongue of minorities living in Hungary as a factor increasing the cohesion of communities, and - wherever so required by the latter -supports the teaching of the vernacular in public educational institutions not belonging to local government of minority settlements, in pursuance of subsections (2) to (4) of this Section and of Sections 44 to 49 of the present Act.

(2)   A child belonging to a minority - depending on the related decision of the parents or of the person who has custody of the child - can be instructed in the vernacular or partly in the vernacular, partly in Hungarian, or only in Hungarian language.

(3)   Instruction both in the vernacular and partly in the vernacular of the minority may take place in minority kindergartens, schools, classes or groups according to the local possibilities and demands.

(4)   If so requested by the parents or legal representatives of at least 8 (eight) school children belonging to one and the same minority, it is mandatory to organize and maintain a minority class or study group.

SECTION   44

Additional costs incurred in the vernacular instruction as outlined in

221

Section 43, are to be covered by the state or by the local government.

SECTION 45

(1)　In the course of the legal regulation of the general public and higher education, in specifying the structure and content of educational activities and in controlling these activities, the specific cultural and educational interests of the cultural autonomy of minorities should be enforced in accordance with the present Act.

(2)　To decrease the handicaps arising from the educational level and opportunities of the Gypsy minority population, special conditions for their schooling may be created.

(3)　Educational institutions of minorities, organized in accordance with subsections (3) to (4) of Section 43, have to provide for the teaching of the respective ethnographic rudiments and the history of the given minority and its motherland, as well as for the proper knowledge of its cultural values and traditions.

SECTION 46

(1)　The local and minority local governments are to cooperate in surveying the demands for minority education and also in the organization of education.

(2)　Training vernacular teachers for the fully or partly vernacular education of minorities is a responsibility of the state.

(3)　Through international agreements too, the state is to ensure that persons belonging to a minority take part in courses in the vernacular which are offered by foreign institutions aimed to foster the given culture, either on full-time or part-time basis or in the form of extension or scientific training.

(4)　To accomplish what is included in subsection (2), the state supports the employment as visiting professors of instructors coming from the respective mother or language countries of minorities.

(5)　Inasmuch as minority persons carry on their studies in countries

222

where there exist universities, colleges and other educational institutions offering courses in their respective mother tongue, diplomas and other certifications earned there should be considered equivalent to their counterparts in the Republic of Hungary with due regard to the related Acts and international agreements.

SECTION 47

Local governments of minority settlements and minority local governments may only take over educational institutions from another body or agency on condition that the quality level of education thus far attained is upheld. The extent of state support allocated to the affected institution cannot be decreased in view of this change.

SECTION 48

(1)   Minority educational institutions may admit school children not belonging to the given minority only if the needs of the   given minority have been met and additional capacity is available. Admission (enrollment) to such schools may take place according to rules made public in advance.

(2)   The teaching of the Hungarian language - in a numbers of hours and at a level necessary to master it - also has to be ensured in a minority educational institution.

(3)   In settlements where inhabitants whose mother tongue is Hungarian or other national or ethnic minorities are in numerical minority, the local government is bound to guarantee the instruction of children whose mother tongue is Hungarian or other minority language fullyor partly in their respective mother tongue pursuant to the provisions of the present Act.

SECTION 49

(1) Minority organizations may pursue activities related to general education and may establish - within the bounds of the related legal provisions institution for that purpose which are entitled to maintain international relations.

(2) The national self-government is entitled to establish and maintain theatres, exhibition facilities in museums, publik collections of nation-wide coverage, minority libraries, publishing houses as well as country-wide minority art and scientific institutions. It may apply for budgetary support for such purposes.

(3)   The supply of literature in the vernacular to minorities is to be secured by the network of minority libraries.

(4)   In settlements where no minority local government has been organized, the responsibility for the supply of the minority language literature falls to the local government of the given settlement.

(5)   The acquisition right of minority public collections is not extended to cover such documents as are required by the effective legal rules for archives to be kept by archives.

SECTION 50

(1)   It is the responsibility of the state to provide for the publication of text-books and for the production of educational appliances.

(2)   The state is to support such activities as:

a)   collection of the material remains of minority cultures, the foundation and development of minority public collections;

b)   publishing of books and periodicals of minorities;

c)   publication of laws and communications of public interest in the minority languages;

d)   observation of religious celebrations and rituals related to minority family events and other religious services in the vernacular of minorities.

CHAPTER VII
Use of minority languages

SECTION 51

(1)   Anyone may use one's mother tongue anywhere and at any

224

time in the Republic of Hungary. The possibility of the free use of minority languages - in cases specified by a separate Act - shall be ensured by the state.

(2)   The free use of the mother tongue in the course of civil, penal as well as administrative proceedings is guaranteed by the related provisions of procedural Act.

SECTION 52

(1)   Representatives belonging to a minority may also use their respective mother tongue in the National Assembly.

(2)   Minority representatives also have the right to use their respective mother tongue in the body of representatives of local governments. In case a contribution was made in one of the minority languages, its Hungarian version or summary is to be attached to the minutes of the session.

(3)   If persons belonging to a minority are living in the given settlement, the body of representatives may have the minutes of the sessions kept or summarized in the minority language as well. In the case of a dispute over the interpretation of the content, the Hungarian version is to be considered authentic.

SECTION 53

In compliance with the requests of the minority local government working within its competence, the local government is bound to see that
a)   its decrees are proclaimed and its announcements are made public - in addition to the Hungarian - in the minority language as well;
b)   forms used in administrative proceedings are also made available in the minority language;
c)   the given minority language is also used - in a form and content identical with the Hungarian - on plates indicating place and street names, sign-boards of public offices, public service agencies and in communications about their functioning.

SECTION 54

In settlements where persons belonging to a minority are also living, in the course of filling the posts in local public service offices and in the appointment of local public officials, it is to be ensured that a person, who has - in addition to the necessary professional qualifications - a proficiency in the given minority language, be employed.

CHAPTER VIII
Financial support of minorities; economic management and assets of minority self-governments

SECTION 55

(1)   Financial support necessary to enforce the rights of minorities living in Hungary is to be provided by the state according to subsections (2) to (4).

(2)   To the extent as defined by the Budgetary Act in force, the state will

a)   provide additional normative support to the maintenance of minority education in kindergartens and in schools with fully or partly vernacular language of instruction;

b)   according to a distribution scheme defined by the National Assembly, provide support to the functioning of the national or ethnic minority local governments and of the organizations of national or ethnic minorities.

(3)   In order to support minorities along with the activities pursued in their interest, in one year from the date the present Act has come into force the National Assembly is to start a National and Ethnic Minority Fund (henceforward: Fund) under the following conditions:

a)   The central state budget forms the source of the Fund;

b)   Expenses incurred in the functioning of the Fund have to be covered from the Fund;

c)   Primarily and decisively, activities promoting the minority interests should be supported from the resources of the Fund, while the support of minority self-governments and other organizations continues to depend on the related decisions of the National Assembly;

d)   The decision-making body of the Fund is the Board of Trustees (Curatorium) headed by that member of the government who is in charge of the national and ethnic minorities. Each of the following bodies, authorities and organizations are to send one delegate, with non transferable commission, to the Board of Trustees: the national self-governments of minorities, political parties which have factions within the National Assembly, the Minister of the Interior, the Minister of Culture and Education, the Finance Minister, and the President of the Office for National and Ethnic Minorities. Inasmuch as a minority falling within the present Act has not formed its national self-government, the representative is to be commissioned jointly by the given minority's associations and other organizations existing on the day of promulgating the Act on the Fund. If this commission has not been given out until the statutory meeting of the Board of Trustees, the Board has to co-opt an outstanding personality belonging to the given minority.

e)   The Board of Trustees makes its decisions by simple majority vote.

(4)   To promote the achievement of objectives outlined in subsection (3) the National Assembly may also raise a foundation (foundations) in which the share of the state budget should not exceed 60 (sixty) per cent.

SECTION 56

Organizations, foundations and private persons, both domestic and foreign, may also contribute to the financial support of minorities. In the case of foreign contributions to the support of minority cultures, the state may provide tariff preferences or relief from customs duties as regulated by separate legal measures,

SECTION   57

The lawful use of financial supports given by the state is to be controlled by the State Audit Office in accordance with legal rules for the use of budgetary resources.

Assets of the minority self-governments

SECTION 58

(1)   To the assets of the local governments of minority settlements - with due regard to differences mentioned in the present Act - regulations concerning the assets of governments have to be applied.

(2)   Minority self-governments may in general obtain finances necessary to their functioning from the following sources:

a)   contributions from the state budget;
b)   contributions from the county or settlement-level self- governments;
c)   their own incomes (including returns on their own ventures);
d)   support from foundations;
e)   support from domestic and foreign organizations;
f)   returns on assets placed at their disposal;
g)   donations.

SECTION 59

(1)   Of the total assets possessed by the local government within its competence, those necessary to the minority local government to perform its duties within its sphere of tasks and authority shall be made available for use by the latter. This transfer, however, must not prevent the local government from carrying out its normal duties.

(2)   To create proper operational conditions for the individual national self-governments of minorities, the locally competent self-government (local government) is bound - with a compensation by the state - to place a separately usable building or part of building of a useful area of 150 to 300 square metres at their disposal in three months from their formation, provided their formation takes place within two budgetary years from the enactment of the present Act.

(3)   To the utilization right and to the transfer procedure, the general rules of legal regulations related to the property of local government are - wherever applicable - to be applied.

(4)   In respect of the normative state contribution, organizations maintained by the local and national self-governments are judged on an equal footing with non-governmental institutions offering human services.

SECTION 60

(1)   Forming part of the property of local governments of minority settlements, minority local governments or of national self-governments (henceforward: minority self-government) are all those assets, movable or immovable, which have been passed - on any legal pretext - into their ownership by legal and private entities, or natural persons.

(2)   In respect of movable and immovable assets handed over to it, the minority self-government has the rights and responsibilities connected with ownership as laid down by legal regulations concerning the acquisition of property through transfer.

(3)   A minority self-government may only take part in enterprises the responsibility of which does not exceed the extent of its contribution in terms of assets.

(4)   Exercising the ownership rights incumbent upon the minority self-governments comes under the exclusive competence of general assembly or the session of the body of representatives.

(5)   In case the minority local government ceases to function, all of its assets, movable or immovable, pass into the ownership of the local government. Should the minority local government be organized anew the local government of the settlement is bound to return its assets equivalent with those taken over previously.

CHAPTER   IX
Closing   provisions

SECTION 61

(1)   In terms of the present Act, qualifying as national or ethnic groups living in Hungary are: Armenians, Bulgarians, Croats, Germans, Greeks,   Gypsies, Poles, Romanians, Ruthenians, Serbs, Slovaks, Slovenes and Ukrainians.

(2)   If a minority other than those listed in subsection (1) wishes to prove that it meets the requirements included in the present Act, at

least 1000 (one thousand) citizens with right to vote of that particular minority group may submit its application as a people's initiative to be regarded as an ethnic group to the President of the National Assembly. During the related proceedings, Act XVII of 1989 on Plebiscite and People's Initiatives shall be applied.

(3) The currently active nationality associations decide independently on their continuance, dissolution or transformation.

SECTION 62

(1)   Involving the ministries and other national authorities concerned in this matter, as well as Commissioners of the Republic_, the government - through the Office for National and Ethnic Minorities - promotes the particular rights and interests of minorities and makes arrangements to create proper conditions for their enforcement.

(2)   In two budgetary years from the date the present Act enters into force the government is bound to raise a "Minority Compensation Fund" of 500 million Forints by each minority as a separate heading in the finance bill. Compensation for provable losses caused by the accommodation of national minority self-governments and - if necessary - of minority local governments to the affected local government should be given to the account of this Fund. To review the applications for such compensations, a committee and local governments should be set up under the chairmanship of the President of the Office for National and Ethnic Minorities, in which the given branch of self-governments should be properly represented.

(3)   At least one in every two years, the government is to review the conditions of minorities living in the Republic of Hungary and to submit a report on its findings to the National Assembly.

SECTION 63

(1)   Provisions included in Act LXV of 1990 and other legal regulations concerning local governments should be applied in harmony with the present Act.

(2)   To subsection (1) of Section I of the Law-decree 19 of 1989 on

the Legal Status of Persons Acknowledged as Refugees, the following point g) is to be added:
"g) are not entitled to and not subject to the rights and duties defined by Act LXXVII of 1993."

(3) The actual number of participants in the Meeting of the National Self-Governments when convoked for the first time is to be determined by the meeting of electors somewhere between 13 (thirteen) and 53 (fifty-five) persons.

(4) To cover their operational costs, the national-level self-governments are to be allotted a non-recurrent grant according to the following distribution:

Gypsies	60 million Forints (Fts.)
Germans	30 million Fts.
Croats	30 million Fts.
Slovaks	30 million Fts.
Romanians	30 million Fts.
Bulgarians	15 million Fts.
Greeks	15 million Fts.
Poles	15 million Fts.
Armenians	15 million Fts.
Ruthenians	15 million Fts.
Serbs	15 million Fts.
Slovenes	15 million Fts-
Ukrainians	15 million Fts.
Total	300 million Fts.

(5) To achieve this, from the marketable part of the state's venture stock, an adequate portion has to be separated in a manner corresponding to the regulations governing the use of compensation coupons.3

(6) National self-governments may cede a certain portion of their assets to the minority local governments, provided this would not bring their functioning into an uncovered position.

SECTION 64

(1)   This Act - except subsections (2) and (3) of Section 20 - enter into force on the 90th day from its promulgation. Subsections (2) and (3) of paragraph 20 will come into force at a date to be determined by a separate law.

(2)   Simultaneously with the present act, Chapter XI of Act LXIV of 1990 on the Election of Local Government Representatives and Mayors is to be replaced by the following regulation with effect from the day of calling the general local government elections to be held in 1994:

CHAPTER XI
Protection of the rights of national and ethnic minorities

SECTION 48

(1)   In order to protect the rights of national and ethnic minorities, provisions made by this Act shall be applied in accordance with the conditions and amendments of the present Chapter.

(2)   If a person proposed as candidate of a given national or ethnic minority announces this capacity of his at the time of opening the list of proposed candidates with a unilateral legal declaration, his or her name is to be entered on the ballot. Upon the candidate's request, his or her name has also to be entered on the ballot in the vernacular form of the given minority.

(3)   On the last day of the election campaign, the Hungarian Radio, the Hungarian Television and the local studios are to provide - apart from the normal electoral briefings - an additional broadcasting time for the candidates of national and ethnic minorities.

SECTION 49

(1)   Should the outcome of the local "small-list" election [see: footnote 2) not bring mandate to any of the minority candidates,

a)   to be established is that number of votes which is equivalent to half of the valid votes cast for a candidate having won a mandate with the least number of votes on the small list;

b)   every minority candidate, who has won a number of votes higher than that established in point a) should have a mandate.

(2)   With the mandate won according to the procedure outlined in subsection (1), the number of members in the body of representatives increases compared to what is determined by Section 8.

SECTION 50

(1)   Under the two-vote election system, in the list election, the minority candidates of the individual constituencies may run separately by each national or ethnic minority, but jointly on a common independent list by each minority. (Henceforward together: minority independent list.)

(2)   To start a minority independent list, it is not necessary to reach the one-forth limit prescribed by Section 29, but on the basis of a minority independent list no list in the capital city can be started.

(3)   A minority candidate of an individual constituency may declare - in at least seventeen days before the election day and in written form - that he or she is not inclined to run on the minority list.
(4)   In the case of list election, names of all candidates of the minority list have to be entered in alphabetical order on the ballot.

(5)   The minority independent list is to obtain mandate according to section (4) of paragraph 45. Of the candidates running on the list, he/she who has won most of the votes in the individual constituency is to obtain the mandate.

(6)   In case no mandate results from the election for candidates of the minority independent list,

a)   the smallest number of votes one has to search which still qualifies for a mandate, and half of this number has to be fixed,
b)   a mandate is obtained by all minority independent lists if they have won votes in a number larger than that determined in point a).

(7)   If a candidate on the minority independent list has been elected representative in the individual constituency, his name must be

removed from the list and be replaced by the name of the candidate who has won the next largest number of votes.

(8)   With the mandate won according to the procedure outlined in subsection (6), the number of members in the body of representatives of the settlement increases compared to what is determined by Section 9.

SECTION 51

(1)   The direct election of minority local government (Henceforward: minority local government election) is to be called by the local electoral committee, and the results also have to be established by it.
The election is to be called fifty days before the election of the local government and is to be held on the same day.
(2)   Minority local government election must be called if so requested by at least five persons who confess to belong to one and the same minority and are permanent residents with right to vote in the given settlement.

(3)   Calling the minority local government election must be initiated in written form in seven days from the calling of the settlement-level local government election. The sample of the form to be used to initiating election is shown in Schedule No. 1

(4)   Any minority in a settlement may only organize one minority local government.

(5)   Election may only be held if there are at least as many candidates as the fixed number of minority representatives to be elected.

SECTION 52

(1)   Qualifying as candidate of a local government of national or ethnic minority is the person who was nominated as minority candidate by at least five of the voters of the given constituency - in accordance with the general rules for nomination.

(2)   Not applicable to the nomination of candidates of a minority local government are subsections (3) and (4) of Section 25, moreover restrictions laid down in subsection (1) of Section 27.

(3) Any voting citizen is eligible to a minority local government who is permanent resident in the given settlement and is inclined to assume the responsibility of representing a minority in a manner defined by the law on the rights of national and ethnic minorities.

SECTION 53

(1) Entitled to participate in the minority local government election in a given settlement are all those having the right to vote in the settlement-level election of local government representatives. A sample of the ballot (voting-paper) is shown in Schedule No.2.

(2) The minority local government election consists of one round only. The election is valid if - out of the total number of registered voters - at least five per cent or at least 100 (one hundred) persons in the case of villages, at least five per cent or at least 500 (five hundred) persons in towns, county-rank towns and in the districts of the capital city have cast valid votes.

(3) Those candidates become representatives in minority local governments who have obtained the most votes compared to all the other eligible candidates.

(4) Candidates scoring an equal number of votes can obtain mandate according to their sequence on the ballot.

(5) A candidate who failed to win one single vote, cannot be representative.

(6) If voters have elected representatives in a number less than the required number of members in the body of the minority local government, the body may also function with this decreased membership until the next election. However, the number of members may not be less than two.

(7) If the results of the direct election do not permit the organization of a minority local government, a newer election - on request by at least five voting citizens - should not be held within one year from the unsuccessful one.

(8)   If the mandate of a representative of the minority   local government expires, he or she has to be replaced by one having obtained the next largest number of votes. For lack of such a candidate, the mandate remains vacant until the next election.

SECTION 54

Deadlines and other closing dates of procedures connected with minority local government elections are to be fixed and made public by the local electoral committee. "

[SECTION 64. continued:]

(3) Subsection (1) of Section 31 of Act LXIII of 1992 on the Protection of Personal Data and on the Publicity of Data of   Public interest is to be replaced by the following provision:
" Section 31 subsection (1) The commissioner of data protection is helped with his work by the Office of Data Protection, the organizational and operational rules of which are to be established by the commissioner of data protection. "

(4) Subsection (1) of Section 36 of Act LXIII of 1992 on the Protection of Personal Data and on the Publicity of Data of Public interest is to be replaced by the following provision:
"Section 36 (1) The commissioner of data protection shall be elected in four months from the day Chapter IV (Sections 23 to 31) of the present Act enters into force."

(5)   The government is authorized to issue a decree detailing the rules connected with the financial implications of this Act.

(6)   The National Electoral Committee is authorized to state its standpoints or opinion about the election-related legal provisions and to issue guide-lines for the execution of the present Act.

SECTION 65

(1)   In the course of the election of local government representatives and mayors, the number of the individual "minority populations is established by means of a special data sheet. The returning board shall

give a separate data sheet to any voter who so requires.

(2)   On this special data sheet, the voter declares the nationality which he or she confesses to belong to. In order to facilitate the acknowledgement of double or multiple national or ethnic bindings, voters may indicate more than one nationality or ethnic group. Text of this data sheet is shown in Schedule No. 3 to the present Act.

(3)   The voter is to put this special data sheet into a separate envelope in the polling-booth, and to put it into a separate ballot-box before the returning board.

(4)   The returning board counts the ballots separately by each of the national or ethnic minorities. Voters indicating two or more minorities should be counted as belonging to each of the minorities indicated.

(5)   The returning board shall put down the number of those belonging to the individual national or ethnic minorities should be put down in separate records by each minority or ethnic group. In compliance with the requirement of secrecy, these records shall be prepared in one copy only and shall not include any listing by name.

(6)   Records prepared separately by each minority are to be signed by the members of the returning board by their own hand. The chairman of the returning board is bound to immediately forward the records, along with the bundled ballots to the local electoral committee. Except members of the local electoral committee and the heads of the electoral working group, no one may look into the records.

(7)   Relying on the records, the local electoral committee establishes exact figures for the voting population of national and ethnic minorities living in the given settlement. Summary records on the results of this work must be prepared in two copies by each minority. The first copy is to be sent to the Budapest and/or regional electoral committee, while the second should be kept locally to facilitate an ex-post statistical control of these aggregated data. Except members of the regional and local electoral committees and the heads of the electoral working group, no one may look into the summary records.

(8)   Relying on the Summary records, the Budapest and the regional electoral committees have to establish the population number of the

individual minorities in Budapest and in the counties, and the results have to be recorded on data sheets in two copies. The first copy is to be sent to the Budapest and county directorates of the Hungarian Central Statistical Office (KSH), while the second should be kept locally. Subsequently, the datasheets are to be controlled, handled and used in accordance with the relevant provisions of the present Act and the Act on Statistics and Data Protection.

(9)   The head of the local electoral working group is bound to preserve the second copies of the summary records and the separate data sheets so that they might be inaccessible to unauthorized persons. After statistical data on the population of the individual national and ethnic minorities have been published, the second copies and the separate data sheets shall be destroyed without delay. The execution of the destruction of these documents is to be controlled ex officio by the Budapest or the county electoral committees.

Arpad Goncz
President of the Republic

Gyorgy Szabad
President of the National Assembly

Schedule No.1 to the Act LXXVII of 1993

Sample for a form of initiating the election of a minority local government within a settlement

To the Local Electoral Committee

.... Name of the settlement

Name of the minority that wishes to organize a minority local
government ....
Name of the initiator ....
Permanent residence ....
Identification mark ....

Initiator's statement on the fact that he or she
has right to vote and on the minority he or
she declares to belong to

....
signature by own hand

Date................................. (Day, month, year)

Schedule No. 2 to the Act LXXVII of 1993

Sample for a ballot to be used in the election of a minority government within a settlement

Name of the settlement................................

Election of minority local government within the settlement
Date.................................... (Day, month, year)

1.   Name of the national or ethnic minority

Candidate's   name

Candidate's   name

Candidate's   name

2.   Name of the national or ethnic minority

Candidate's   name

Candidate's   name

Candidate's   name

3.   Name of the national or ethnic minority

Candidate's   name

Candidate's   name

Candidate's   name

Vote may be cast for only one minority, and within this for not more than ....candidates.
Vote for more than one minority invalidates the ballot.
Vote for more candidates than the possible number of representatives to be elected invalidates the ballot.
To mark the vote for a particular minority and the chosen candidate(s), the voter has to cross , with x or +, the answer circle next to the names.

240

Data sheet for the anonymous polling of the population number of the individual national and ethnic minorities

Considering the possible choices listed below and on the basis of your mother tongue, the language most frequently used in your family, and of the cultural values and traditions which you highly esteem and consider as being closely related to you, which of the national minority (minorities) or ethnic group(s) do you, as a Hungarian citizen, declare to belong to?

Armenian
Bulgarian
Croat
German
Greek
Gypsy (Romany)
Hungarian +
Polish
Romanian
Ruthenian
Serb
Slovak
Slovene
Ukrainian

+ The denotation "Hungarian" appears here only to make one possible to declare one's ethnic binding both to a minority and to the majority nation, or to express one's multiple national or ethnic binding.

If you feel to belong to more minorities, you may make several marks.
The use of this data sheet is made possible under Section 65 Act LXXVII of 1993 on the Rights of National and Ethnic Minorities. The above list of national and ethnic minorities includes those listed in the mentioned Act. This data sheet will be processed without indicating any name pursuant to regulations laid down in Section 65 of Act LXXVII of 1993 on the Rights of National and Ethnic Minorities and in the Act on Data Protection and Statistics.

241

NOTES

1 The present law was passed by the Hungarian National Assembly on its session of 7 July 1993.

2 Local "small-list" elections: a kind of local government elections based on a sort of "straight ticket", when all candidates are listed in alphabetical order, and the voter is supposed to vote for only as many candidates as can be representatives in the given settlement. The number of possible representatives is fixed by law.

3 The "Commissioner of Republic" is a government official who is in charge of ensuring the observance of law and legality in general in an administrative unit (county, town, district or other), also acting as a mediator between the government and the given administrative unit.

4 "Compensation coupons" are securities issued by the state in partial compensation for properties (land or other real estates, factories, houses and other assets) confiscated or nationalised prior to 1949 and later during the communist regime.